KAT

ASHMORE'S mission is to empower hungry readers everywhere to feed themselves and their loved ones well and have fun doing it. In Ashmore's debut cookbook, *Big Bites*, she shares 110 wholesome, comforting, and mostly gluten-free recipes that are full of flavor, nourishment, and joy—meant to be devoured in big bites! With her signature personality and excitement, this is a celebration of nature and seasonality, and encourages home cooks to rethink familiar ingredients. From "Hungry Lady Salads" and weeknight dinners to snacks and desserts, *Big Bites* shares recipes for Shaved Caesar Salad with Fennel and Crispy Chickpeas, BLT Wedge Salad with Croutons and Creamy Basil Dressing, honey mustard roasted salmon, Salt and Vinegar Smashed Potatoes, Five-Minute Tzatziki, Orange Ricotta Company Cake, and more! Bring fun back into your kitchen with Kat Ashmore and *Big Bites*.

BIG
BITES

BIG BITES

KAT ASHMORE

WHOLESOME, COMFORTING RECIPES THAT ARE BIG ON FLAVOR, NOURISHMENT, AND FUN

RODALE
NEW YORK

Published in the United States by Rodale Books, an imprint of Random House,
a division of Penguin Random House LLC, New York.

RodaleBooks.com | RandomHouseBooks.com

RODALE and the Plant colophon are registered
trademarks of Penguin Random House LLC.

Library of Congress Cataloging-in-Publication Data

Names: Ashmore, Kat, author.

Title: Big bites / Kat Ashmore.

Description: New York : Rodale, [2024] | Includes index.

Identifiers: LCCN 2023004357 (print) | LCCN 2023004358 (ebook)
| ISBN 9780593580158 (hardcover) | ISBN 9780593580165 (ebook)

Subjects: LCSH: Quick and easy cooking. | LCGFT: Cookbooks.

Classification: LCC TX833.5 .A85 2024 (print) | LCC TX833.5 (ebook)
| DDC 641.5/12--dc23/eng/20230210

LC record available at https://lccn.loc.gov/2023004357

LC ebook record available at https://lccn.loc.gov/2023004358

ISBN 978-0-593-58015-8

Ebook ISBN 978-0-593-58016-5

Printed in China

Book and cover design by Laura Palese
Photographs by Christine Han

10 9 8 7 6 5 4 3 2 1

First Edition

FOR MY FATHER,

✳

who fed my soul with
encouragement,
humor, and unconditional
love. Your seat is
forever saved at my table.

CONTENTS

SOUPS + STEWS

SUNDAY SUPPERS

VEGGIES + SIDES

DESSERT MENU

SECRET WEAPONS

INTRODUCTION

IT ALL STARTED WITH A SALAD.

*W*ell, that's not quite where it *all* started for the twelve-year-old girl who was reading cookbooks before bed like novels, but it's where this book, *Big Bites*, started. I've wanted to write a book for years—in culinary school, while working in food at Martha Stewart—but I felt that I would simply be jumping into a conversation that didn't require my input. There were so many amazing cookbooks out there, what was I going to say that really mattered? I knew that I'd feel excited writing it, but *why* I was writing it felt more self-serving than community serving at the time. So, I waited, until now.

The desire—no, the need—to write this book came to me in January of 2022 when my Hungry Lady Salads broke loose on the internet.

With the New Year, New You haze on the horizon, I knew what you were thinking. I knew, because I am you. I am hungry, not just physically but emotionally and mentally, for food that makes me feel something: big bowls of slurpable noodles, crackling chicken skin, creamy salad dressing, and comforting crumb cakes. I also want to feel good in my body and thoughtful in my eating. I want to be healthy and well fed—is that so much to ask? Dreading the onset of January as the traditional month of deprivation, I was inspired to create a series of big meal-in-a-bowl, have-to-eat-it-with-a-large-spoon salads. My approach to food is about what we can add to our plates, not what we "should" take away. These salads weren't dainty—they were hearty, meant to be devoured in big bites, and again the next day, and again the day after that because they just kept getting better. I called them Hungry Lady Salads and TikTok exploded. My audience steadily and quickly grew as you begged for more Hungry Lady Salads and eventually Hungry Lady Soups, and started using this language with excitement and pride. Not only was it okay to be hungry—it

THESE
RECIPES ARE
ABUNDANT,
NOT
RESTRICTIVE.
CREATIVE,
NOT FUSSY.

was *fun*. I receive messages daily from worn-out moms and busy home cooks saying that my approach and recipes have made you fall in love with cooking again, that your families wouldn't touch kale and now ask for my Tuscan Kale Salad with Lemon Tahini Dressing (page 109) weekly, that you no longer buy salad dressings and order takeout. You tell me that you made one of my desserts for a party and everyone begged for the recipe. You tell me that your burly, carnivore husband asked for three bowls of veggie-packed soup. You tell me that my food has helped you feel more nourished, more satisfied, more creative. I knew I was onto something—healthy food for food *lovers*, and my mission became even more clear. I knew it was time to write my first cookbook.

Did I set out to produce a beautiful, high-quality cookbook? Yes. But make no mistake, I want you to make a mess of this book. That's right, mess it up right along with your favorite kitchen apron that you reach for time and time again because it feels good and has seen you through so many kitchen adventures. I want *Big Bites* to become a mainstay in your kitchen, dog-eared and coffee-stained and reached for every time you need a recipe for dinner, a cake to bring to brunch, a casserole for a sick friend. With this book, my mission is to empower hungry readers everywhere to serve yourselves and your families well, and have fun doing it. These are simple, stress-free recipes and strategies you will love making and eating, sharing big bites of personality and joy. These recipes are abundant, not restrictive. Creative, not fussy. Thoughtful, not complicated. These are recipes to feel proud to serve and proud to eat.

I suppose you might call me a "flexitarian," as I don't completely exclude any foods from my diet, but I am keenly aware of what makes me feel my best and what does not, so I let that guide me 90 percent of the time. My training is as a chef, not a dietician, so making amazing-tasting food always comes first. My recipes are trustworthy and reliable, and infused with years of training and technique. I encourage home cooks, especially moms on a self-love journey, to focus on what we are adding to our plate rather than taking away. Because my goal is to make recipes that anyone can make, I offer lots of variation with dairy-free, gluten-free, vegan options and the like. I don't want anyone to feel left behind. Whole foods are beautiful, and with a little finesse and creativity, everyone at the table will be excited to eat them. Just ask my husband, who swore he hated brussels sprouts and now eats them with pleasure. The first time I served them, piled high in a heap under a spicy caramel glaze, he expected the gray-ish mush boiled to oblivion that gave them a bad rap for so many of us. Turns out, he quite likes brussels sprouts and all other veggies too. My motto is if you think you don't like vegetables, you're eating them the wrong way.

My cooking is a celebration of nature and the seasons and encourages home cooks to rethink familiar ingredients. Beautiful food does not need to be complicated; it just has to be considered and thoughtful. More than anything, I want readers to be inspired by my recipes, to make them and love them, so I'll always offer substitutions should they be of better use within a particular lifestyle. I believe in green smoothies and cinnamon rolls, sometimes at the same time, and that true wellness is about balance and inclusion. No food is "clean" and no food is "dirty." Make the most of the real, plentiful food that is all around us, and take big bites of it. That is my food religion.

I don't come from a family of elaborate cooks so much as a family of enthusiastic eaters. In fact, most of my treasured childhood memories revolve around food. I remember running around our neighborhood in the rain with my father, competing over who could jump into the biggest puddle. We returned home, soaking wet, and my mother wrapped me in a towel so we could all eat steaming bowls of homemade macaroni and cheese. I don't remember a perfectly juicy Thanksgiving turkey, but I do remember my brother and I chasing each other with black olives (canned, always) on our fingers and thumb-wrestling for the bigger half of the wishbone. I felt free to play with food, and associated food with feeling supremely loved. Big bites, big laughs, and big love.

As I grew into my teen years, my fascination with food turned into a fascination with creating food. I would insist on bringing half a dozen cookbooks on family vacations, much to my luggage-carrying father's chagrin, and read them like novels before bed. One might say I was a bit obsessed. One would certainly say I still am.

Flash forward to July 2020. I had been a stay-at-home mother for three years (my kids were one and three years old) and I was struggling without a creative outlet. I'll be honest: I wasn't a very good stay-at-home mom. I'd always tremendously valued what I was creating and producing professionally, and I didn't realize how much that part of me impacted my self-esteem, my self-respect, and my overall happiness. I'd left my career as a corporate recipe developer and producer to care for my children, and as the newborn haze started to clear I looked around and barely recognized myself. I was anxious, overwhelmed, and lonely. I was burdened by weight, emotionally and physically, and longed for a purpose that had nothing to do with being a mom. My passion for food hadn't waned, but in the absence of a way to channel my creative energy, I'd turned all my passion into eating. And eating. And eating. I told you, food has always had a bit of a hold on me, sometimes

WELCOME TO THE BIG BITES CLUB.

feeling like a hug and sometimes feeling like shackles. I made the fateful decision to launch a healthy recipe blog and start a TikTok account and put my passion for food to good use.

Having worked for large corporations, where my production and development roles were specific and delineated, it became clear that I had a lot to learn when it came to being an entrepreneur. I had a lot to learn about wearing all the hats at once. My first videos were of helpful kitchen tips, like how to choose a ripe watermelon at the supermarket, and how to get the most juice out of a lemon. I didn't know exactly what people wanted to see, so I focused on really listening to what people responded to, what pain points they had, and let that lead the way.

I watched in amazement as a community began to form around my videos and more specifically around the food and how it made them feel. I started walking taller and laughing louder and feeling more energized than I had in years. I woke up excited and motivated, and I felt like I was offering something valuable—but I was getting something so valuable out of it too. The videos and interaction with this community has been an act of self-care— every day, putting myself out there and sharing my love for food, along with the passion I brought to what I made, what I ate, the food I nourished my family with, let me rediscover a spark that had almost gone out. To know that I've played a part in your healing your family's idea of what "healthy" food is is an honor and responsibility I don't take lightly. The big headfake is, I've been healing right along with you.

Big Bites is about simple, comforting recipes that portray "healthy food" in a whole new way. Food that is abundant in colors, textures, nourishment, and flavor. Big bites of big food that is salty, chewy, crunchy, sweet, creamy, and full of personality. This is a book about falling in love with real food, and in turn, maybe falling in love with yourself.

For so many, even me, cooking every day for a family can feel burdensome. If you feel a sense of dread as you stare down the dinner hour, it's not too late to change your approach. I believe wholeheartedly that we all have the agency to create a loving relationship with ourselves, and that healthy, delicious food can be a way to do that daily. I'll be sharing hearty, abundant, voluptuous food that just happens to be good for you, and encouraging home cooks to shake things up and cook real food with enthusiasm. There are so many "I can't believe I made that" moments waiting for you in this book.

Welcome to the Big Bites Club.

THE BIG BITES PANTRY

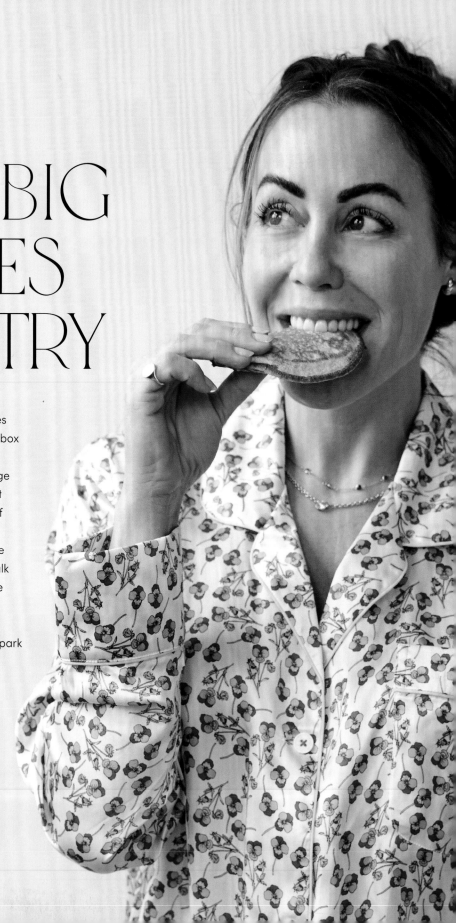

The ingredients you use are what makes your dish. I don't mean that in the soapbox "use only organic, grass-fed, blah blah blah," way, but that there is a wide range in flavor and quality in every ingredient category that will affect the outcome of your recipe. If you want to know about substitutions for these recipes, this is the place. To set you up for success, let's talk about what I mean when I call for these frequently used ingredients and what swaps you can (and maybe shouldn't) make. I want you knocking it out of the park with Every. Single. Recipe.

SALT

I use two kinds of salt in my everyday cooking and baking.

* *Kosher salt*   I use Diamond Crystal kosher salt, which is half as salty as Morton's. I know, that's significant. Diamond is the standard salt in most restaurants, and its delicate salt crystals allow you to have more control over the saltiness of your dish. If you're using Morton's in your kitchen, use half as much salt as I call for in each recipe.

* *Flaky sea salt*   Maldon is my go-to for a flaky salt that is used to finish everything from crispy chicken to blondies. Jacobsen also makes an excellent flaky sea salt, and I happen to carry a small tin in my purse at all times for when I eat out and the food needs a little "something." Ninety-five percent of the time, that "something" is salt. Iodized table salt is not recommended in my recipes.

PEPPER

If you don't already own a pepper grinder and some black peppercorns, I urge you to get them. The pre-ground stuff is miles away from the piquant, subtly floral flavor of freshly cracked pepper. If you use as much pepper as I do, grind some weekly in a clean coffee grinder and keep it, covered, next to your kosher salt on your counter. See that? Just as easy as the pre-ground kind and so, so much better.

OILS

There are a few oils I use regularly in my kitchen and call for frequently in this book.

* *Olive oil*   You don't realize how much you use an ingredient until you write a cookbook. Turns out, I use more olive oil than I would have even guessed. I keep two extra-virgin varieties on hand at all times—one affordable workhorse (Whole Foods 365 brand is my go-to) to use for roasting, baking, and salad dressings, and then one more expensive oil for finishing only. I'm partial to Italian and Spanish olive oils for this special use, though California is turning out some great oils right now as well. Oh, and please don't keep your oils next to the stove, where they are subject to residual heat every time you turn it on. Protect those oils!

* *Neutral oil*   When I call for a neutral oil, I'm asking for an oil whose composition won't do much to affect the flavor of the dish and one that usually has a higher smoke point than olive oil. For example, we don't want a strong super-grassy extra-virgin olive oil in sweet baked goods because it will alter the flavor. While I'm not averse to using canola or vegetable oil, and sometimes do, I usually use sunflower or safflower oils as my neutral oils. They are a bit more expensive than the former, and less processed. Use whatever is in your price range and accessible to you.

✳ *Coconut oil*   I use virgin, refined coconut oil most often in my recipes. It behaves a lot like butter in baked goods and is a great way to achieve a tender crumb without using dairy.

Refined coconut oil has very little coconut taste, so if you want a more pronounced coconut flavor, use unrefined. I buy mine in bulk at Costco, and since it comes in a clear container I keep it in a dark cabinet away from the sun. It is shelf stable for what feels like ages, and will last for a good long time.

FLOUR

I use all sorts of flours in my cooking and baking, but the ones you will see here most often are gluten-free all-purpose flour, almond flour, and oat flour. No, I am not gluten-free, though I do eat gluten only about ten percent of the time, as I feel better that way. I don't believe in all or nothing in terms of gluten, or dairy, or sugar . . . You get the picture.

✳ *Gluten-free all-purpose flour*   First thing's first—you can always substitute regular all-purpose flour for any recipe where I call for gluten-free all-purpose.

Bob's Red Mill 1-1 Baking Flour is almost always what I use in baked goods recipes. I find it mimics regular all-purpose flour the best of any brand I've tried. Cup 4 Cup is also amazing, though pricier. King Arthur makes a good gluten-free flour blend that is heartier than the first two, so I use that when I want a dense crumb or am dredging fish or poultry or thickening a sauce.

✳ *Almond flour*   Here I'm referring to blanched almond flour, where the skins of the almonds have been removed. It will be lighter in texture and color than almond meal and look a bit like sand (thankfully it doesn't taste like it). I use almond flour often in baking as a component to the flour base as it provides bulk and moisture with the fat content of the almonds. I buy mine in bulk from Costco and put the bag right in the refrigerator—always refrigerate or freeze almond flour to avoid the almond oil going rancid and to make it last a long time.

✳ *Oat flour*   I have quite literally never purchased oat flour as I make my own at home. You can of course buy, but all it takes is putting old-fashioned rolled oats in a blender or food processor and blitzing for 10 to 20 seconds to get oat flour for pennies on the dollar.

YOGURT

As I like to tailor recipes for all sorts of lifestyles and dietary preferences, you will see both cow's milk yogurt and dairy-free yogurt included in this book. If you're using cow's milk yogurt, Greek included, full fat is always the best bet and it's what I recommend. For dairy-free yogurt, So Delicious Unsweetened Coconut Yogurt is my preferred yogurt, as the coconut taste is very mild and it takes well to savory and sweet flavors alike. It's also widely available at grocery stores. Dairy-free and regular cow's milk yogurt are largely interchangeable in these recipes—just know that if you're using dairy-free in place of cow's milk Greek yogurt, you will be missing some viscosity and richness that only full-fat cow's milk Greek yogurt provides.

MILK

Just as with yogurt, non-dairy and cow's milk are largely interchangeable in these recipes. Unsweetened almond and oat milk are my go-tos for non-dairy milks; I never use sweetened milk, as I like to control the sugar in my recipes and sometimes I want to use them in savory preparations like sauces and soups. I often make a quick vegan buttermilk just as I do regular buttermilk by adding a teaspoon of vinegar to a cup of plant-based milk—it's that easy.

MUSTARD

Mustard is a must. I'm actually surprised I've never used that pun before. I use it constantly in my kitchen in everything from sauces and salad dressings to a coating for fish and chicken. It adds so much flavor without any effort and cuts through fat nicely to wake up the flavor of a dish. I use Dijon mustard daily (specifically Grey Poupon or Maille) and that is what I call for again and again in this book, whole grain mustard often, and French's Classic Yellow Mustard for hot dogs, Easter ham, and corned beef. Old habits die hard.

EGGS

Eggs are always large eggs in my kitchen and in my recipes unless otherwise noted. When I call for room temperature eggs in baked goods recipes, don't panic that you didn't prepare well enough. Place cold eggs in a bowl of hot water while you gather the rest of your ingredients and you'll have room temperature eggs in minutes.

GARLIC

When I call for garlic, it's always fresh garlic, unless I am calling for garlic powder. If you follow me on social media, you aren't surprised by my dogged view on this. The jarred stuff is not only more expensive than fresh, but it's heavily processed and has lost almost all of its flavor swishing around in water for who knows how long. If chopping garlic each time you cook is too laborious, process multiple heads at a time in a food processor and freeze it in teaspoon size, breaking off pieces as you need it for cooking. One teaspoon is about one clove.

BUTTER

While I use olive oil much more than I use butter, I do love butter and call for it in a number of recipes. I use unsalted butter in my recipes because I like controlling the amount of salt that goes into my food. I keep my butter on the counter, covered, at room temperature, making it easy to throw into finished pastas and rice. Butter is not dairy-free, due to the milk solids, so if this is a restriction you have, use a quality vegan butter such as Miyokos.

STOCK

Good soup starts with good stock. I don't make the rules, I just play by them. So, what is good stock? I always make homemade stock and keep lots of it in my freezer, which is why I included the recipe for Scrappy Slow-Cooker Chicken Stock (page 165) in this book. It is the foundation of almost every single soup I make. Because my homemade stock is unsalted, I can control how much salt goes into each recipe. If you're using salted, store-bought stock, you'll need to take that into account and resist salting your recipe until the end, if needed. There are some quality stocks available now and I think Better Than Bouillon is a great thing to have on hand. I have their Beef Bouillon jar in my fridge as we speak, since cartons of beef stock often contain almost no beef at all.

NUTS AND SEEDS

I do love crunch. You will find nuts and seeds called for often in these recipes, especially in salads. Toasting nuts brings out their flavor, and you can either purchase them already roasted or toast them yourself. To toast, simply place them in a dry skillet over medium heat and toss them around for a few minutes until they have browned and start to let off a nutty aroma. Keep an eye on them so they don't burn. I discourage you from using seasoned nuts as, again, I want you in control of how much salt is in your dish. Do you see a pattern here?

PASTA

I am certain that my Italian ancestors would have a lot to say about my adoration for brown rice pasta. We eat pasta of some sort weekly in my home and I simply feel better when I'm eating this variety, specifically Jovial Foods brand, which is available widely now at grocery stores and is my go-to pasta in all shapes from spaghetti to penne and fusilli. Regular pasta can always be used in these recipes with no change in the outcome whatsoever.

GRAINS AND LEGUMES

✳ *Legumes*   If it were 2001 and I was naming my brand after a food, it would probably have "chickpea" in the name. Where do I even start? Legumes are a security blanket for me: if I have a can of chickpeas or beans in the pantry, I know I have dinner. Sometimes I cook them from scratch, often in the slow cooker, when they are really going to be a main event for a large group, but most often in my daily life I open a can from the pantry just like you.

✳ *Grains*   Grains are worthy of much more than their role as "that thing in sushi you dip in soy sauce." I celebrate grains in all their glory, and the Saffron Rice Bake with Chickpeas, Tomatoes, and Loads of Garlic (page 198) is an example of that. Farro, barley, quinoa, and rice are staples in my kitchen, and I think they should be in yours too. There is a lot of variance in how long to cook the many different types, so pay attention to the kind you are buying and follow the directions on the package. You'll get the hang of it quite quickly.

SUGARS

In terms of sugar, I'm on the reduction track. I don't demonize it and I don't exalt it. I understand and appreciate its true role in our food and I know how to use and consume it responsibly. That was not always the case, believe me, but it is now.

✳ *Refined sugars*   The sweet recipes in this book sometimes use granulated sugar, and when they do, it's because it is the best sugar for that recipe. I am always challenging myself to see how much sugar I can withhold without affecting the integrity of a recipe and what unique interest I can add to compensate for it. Demerara, or turbinado sugar, is what I use for finishing some baked goods like muffins and quickbreads. Yes, it is less processed than granulated, but that's not why I use it. I use it because of its beauty, large crystal texture, and ability to make even humble muffins look like they came from a bakery.

✳ *Unrefined sugars*   Maple syrup and coconut sugar are two other sugars I use often, and when I want a deep caramel flavor in a recipe. Maple syrup is always pure maple syrup, not pancake syrup, which is nothing like the real stuff.

Coconut sugar is found at most grocery stores and online, but it can be substituted with light or dark brown sugar in most recipes if that's what you have.

MORNING
PERSON

AVOCADO TOAST WITH HOT HONEY AND GREENS

MAKES 1 SERVING

1   slice hearty sandwich bread
    (such as sourdough, whole-wheat,
    or multigrain)

½   medium ripe avocado

    Juice of ½ lime

¼   teaspoon red pepper flakes

1   tablespoon honey

¼   cup tender lettuces (such as field
    greens or arugula microgreens)

    Flaky sea salt for serving

If you've never had the sublime combination of avocado, honey, and chili, this is your nudge to try it. It's at once creamy, cool, spicy, and sweet. Piled onto crunchy bread with a generous hit of flaky salt, it rivals the trendiest avocado toast in Los Angeles, and you won't have paid twelve dollars for it.

To make this easy to throw together throughout the week, you can prepare a big batch of the chili-infused honey by combining 1 cup of honey with 2 teaspoons of red pepper flakes; store it at room temperature in a lidded container.

1   Toast the bread.

2   In a small bowl, combine the avocado and lime juice and mash with a fork.

3   In another small bowl, combine the red pepper flakes and honey and microwave for 15 to 30 seconds until hot.

4   Cover the toasted bread with the greens, top with the mashed avocado, and drizzle with the hot honey.

5   Sprinkle with flaky salt and serve.

EGGS IN PURGATORY *WITH* GARLIC TOASTS

MAKES 3 TO 6 SERVINGS

Extra-virgin olive oil

3 large garlic cloves, 2 thinly sliced and 1 halved

⅛ teaspoon red pepper flakes

1 teaspoon balsamic vinegar

1 (28-ounce) can whole peeled tomatoes, preferably San Marzano

Kosher salt

¼ teaspoon freshly cracked black pepper

4 tablespoons chiffonade (sliced into ribbons) fresh basil

4 tablespoons freshly grated Parmesan cheese

6 large eggs

Sliced crusty bread for serving

This is for all of my savory-breakfast people. Many cultures have a version of this dish, in which eggs are gently cooked in a savory tomato sauce and served with bread. Think of this as the Italian version of shakshuka. The balsamic vinegar is not traditional, though I like the punch it adds to the sauce. The eggs and sauce are made in one pan, with minimal effort, and can be taken straight from stovetop to table, making this a beautifully rustic main course for brunch.

1 In a large cast-iron skillet with a lid, heat 2 tablespoons of olive oil over medium heat. Add the sliced garlic and red pepper flakes and cook just until the garlic turns golden brown at the edges, about 1 minute. Add the balsamic and stir for 10 seconds before adding the tomatoes, ½ teaspoon of salt, the pepper, and 2 tablespoons of the basil, then turn the heat to medium-low.

2 Simmer, covered, for 15 minutes until the mixture is slightly thickened and the flavors have melded. Using a potato masher or heavy spoon, mash the tomatoes into a sauce and stir in 2 tablespoons of the Parmesan.

3 Using the back of a spoon, immediately make six divots in the tomato sauce, then crack an egg into each divot. Cover the pan again and let cook until the eggs are set to taste, 2 to 3 minutes for runny yolks and 3 to 5 minutes for medium yolks.

4 While the eggs are cooking, toast the bread in a toaster or under the broiler. Rub the warm toast with the halved garlic clove, drizzle with olive oil, and sprinkle with salt.

5 To serve, sprinkle the eggs with the remaining 2 tablespoons of Parmesan and 2 tablespoons of basil.

6 Place a piece of toast in each shallow bowl and spoon the eggs and sauce over the top. Serve immediately.

MAPLE CORN MUFFINS WITH RASPBERRY CHIA JAM

MAKES 12 MUFFINS

1¼ cups fine yellow cornmeal

1 cup oat flour

1 teaspoon baking powder

1 teaspoon baking soda

1 teaspoon kosher salt

⅓ cup neutral oil

¼ cup maple syrup

2 large eggs, room temperature

1 cup unsweetened almond milk

1 teaspoon apple cider vinegar

Raspberry Chia Jam (opposite) for serving

Most of us hear "corn muffins" and think of the bread that goes with a big steaming bowl of chili, or at least I used to. After making these muffins for years, I am now most excited about them for breakfast, especially paired with this easy reduced-sugar raspberry jam. The muffins are slightly sweet, with a hearty oat flour base paired with cornmeal for texture. I like to use a 2 ounce ice cream scoop for easy and even portioning. They freeze beautifully too, meaning a nutritious breakfast bite can always be at the ready.

1 Preheat the oven to 350°F.

2 Spray a standard 12-cup muffin tin with nonstick cooking spray or line with cupcake liners.

3 In a medium bowl, whisk together the cornmeal, oat flour, baking powder, baking soda, and salt. In a separate bowl, combine the oil, maple syrup, eggs, almond milk, and apple cider vinegar.

4 Make a well in the center of the dry ingredients and pour the wet ingredients into the center of the well. Gently fold to combine using a rubber spatula.

5 Divide the batter evenly among the baking cups, using about ¼ cup of batter per cavity.

6 Bake for 16 to 20 minutes, until the muffins are puffed up, golden, and just baked through. An inserted toothpick should come out clean.

7 Let the muffins cool for 10 minutes before serving with the jam. Store the muffins covered at room temperature for up to 3 days, or freeze for up to 3 months.

RASPBERRY CHIA JAM

Makes 1½ cups

1   pound frozen raspberries

2   tablespoons maple syrup

1   teaspoon lemon juice

¼   teaspoon kosher salt

2   tablespoons chia seeds

In a medium pot set over medium heat, combine the raspberries, maple syrup, lemon juice, and salt. Simmer for 5 to 7 minutes, using a spoon to help the fruit break down.

Add the chia seeds and cook for another minute. It's okay if the jam looks runny; it will thicken as it cools. Let it cool to room temperature before transferring to a glass or plastic container with a lid. The jam will keep for up to 1 week in the fridge.

NEW YORK–STYLE CRUMB CAKE

MAKES ONE 8-INCH SQUARE CAKE

CRUMB TOPPING

- ⅔ cup gluten-free all-purpose flour
- ⅓ cup coconut sugar or brown sugar
- 1 teaspoon ground cinnamon
- ¼ teaspoon kosher salt
- ⅔ cup walnuts, chopped
- ⅓ cup coconut oil, melted

CAKE

- ¼ cup coconut oil, melted and cooled
- ½ cup granulated sugar
- 2 large eggs, room temperature
- 1 cup unsweetened plain coconut yogurt
- 2 teaspoons vanilla extract
- 1½ cups gluten-free all-purpose flour
- 1½ teaspoons baking powder
- ½ teaspoon baking soda
- ½ teaspoon kosher salt
- Confectioners' sugar for dusting

This is a lighter take on those sky-high crumb cakes you see in every corner deli in Manhattan. Brown sugar crumbs the size of gumballs set atop moist, buttery cake all resting under a snowstorm of confectioners' sugar. I salivate just thinking about it. Do *not* sleep on this cake. It looks identical to a proper New York crumb cake, but is gluten- and dairy-free.

The New York deli certainly didn't invent the crumb cake, but they helped put it on the map in an accessible way by offering individual slices wrapped in cling film ready to snow all over your shirt as you race to the next taxi. This cake will be the best thing you get on your shirt for a long time to come.

1 **TO MAKE THE CRUMB TOPPING:** In a medium bowl, use a fork to mix the flour, sugar, cinnamon, salt, and walnuts.

2 Stream in the coconut oil and mix with a spatula until it resembles damp sand. Refrigerate the topping until you are ready to bake the cake.

3 **TO MAKE THE CAKE:** Preheat the oven to 350°F. Spray an 8-inch square baking pan with nonstick cooking spray and line with parchment paper, leaving an overhang on two sides for easy removal.

4 In the bowl of a standing mixer, or using a bowl and hand mixer, combine the coconut oil and sugar and beat together for 30 seconds. Add the eggs, yogurt, and vanilla and beat until smooth.

5 To the bowl with the wet ingredients, add the flour, baking powder, baking soda, and salt. Mix until there are no clumps of flour remaining. Transfer the batter to the prepared pan and smooth the top.

6 Remove the crumb topping from the fridge and scatter it in large pieces over the batter evenly, starting around the edges and working inward. It will look like a lot of topping, and it is!

7 Bake for 40 to 45 minutes, until a toothpick comes out just clean. The topping may still look a bit wet in the middle, but it will harden as it rests.

8 Let the cake cool in the pan for 15 minutes, then lift it out with the parchment sling and transfer to a wire rack to cool completely. Sprinkle with the confectioners' sugar and serve.

ONE-BOWL PUMPKIN BANANA BUNDT CAKE

MAKES 10 TO 12 SERVINGS ✳ 1 BUNDT CAKE

2	cups gluten-free all-purpose flour
1	cup oat flour
1	teaspoon baking soda
2	teaspoons baking powder
1	teaspoon kosher salt
1½	teaspoons ground cinnamon
½	teaspoon ground ginger
½	teaspoon ground nutmeg
3	large eggs, room temperature
1	teaspoon vanilla extract
½	cup extra-virgin olive oil
1	cup maple syrup
1	(15-ounce) can unsweetened pumpkin puree
2	very ripe medium bananas, mashed
1	cup chopped toasted walnuts (optional)

This is the cake for anyone who is hesitant about baking, and is an absolute staple in my house each fall. The ingredients list isn't short, but the cake itself is simple to make and requires very little cleanup, as it all comes together in one bowl. You can use 2½ teaspoons of pumpkin pie spice instead of the cinnamon, ginger, and nutmeg if you have that on hand. The banana, olive oil, and heady amount of pumpkin puree guarantee an incredibly moist cake, and one that is practically impossible to screw up. A nostalgic fog of cozy aromas will fill your kitchen as it bakes, leaving you to feel delightfully domestic despite the little effort you've spent making it.

1 Preheat the oven to 350°F and spray a standard Bundt pan with nonstick spray. Set aside.

2 In a large bowl, whisk together the flours, baking soda, baking powder, salt, cinnamon, ginger, and nutmeg.

3 Fold in the eggs, vanilla, oil, and maple syrup and whisk until smooth.

4 Add the pumpkin and bananas and mix again for 10 to 20 seconds to combine and until there are no traces of flour remaining. If you are using walnuts, fold them into the batter now with a rubber spatula.

5 Transfer the batter to the prepared pan and bake for 50 to 55 minutes until a tester comes out just clean.

6 Let the cake sit for 10 minutes in the pan before turning it over onto a wire rack to cool completely. Cut and serve, or store at room temperature until ready to serve. It will keep, tightly wrapped, for about 5 days.

OVERNIGHT COCONUT CREAM PIE OATS

MAKES 4 SERVINGS

8 ounces full-fat coconut milk

2 cups unsweetened almond milk

¼ cup maple syrup

1 teaspoon vanilla extract

1½ cups old-fashioned oats

⅓ cup chia seeds

¼ teaspoon kosher salt

⅛ teaspoon ground cinnamon

¼ cup toasted shredded unsweetened coconut for serving (optional)

If you're an aspiring meal-prepper, overnight oats are a sensible place to start. They ask for only five minutes before a sleep in the fridge to transform into a creamy, nutrient-packed breakfast all week long. These oats are my very favorite rendition, made with fragrant coconut milk, a generous dose of vanilla, a warm hit of cinnamon, and toasted coconut for crunch. I use 16-ounce lidded glass jars for portioning these, and serve them that way too. If you are as seduced by coconut as I am, they will soon become a favorite of yours as well.

1 When portioning out the coconut milk, open the can and add the 8 ounces to a large mixing bowl. If the hard cream and water are separated, ensure you get some of both in there. Whisk for 10 to 20 seconds if needed to combine the two into a creamy milk.

2 Add the almond milk, maple syrup, vanilla, oats, chia seeds, salt, and cinnamon. Whisk briefly until well combined.

3 Divide among four 16-ounce jars, cover, and refrigerate overnight.

4 Serve topped with toasted coconut, or with berries when they are in season. The oats will keep in the refrigerator for 5 to 7 days.

SECRET INGREDIENT FRITTATA

2   tablespoons extra-virgin olive oil

1   small onion, thinly sliced

16   ounces button mushrooms, sliced

3   packed cups fresh spinach

¼   teaspoon kosher salt

10   large eggs

¼   cup milk

½   cup grated aged Cheddar cheese

2   tablespoons finely chopped fresh herbs (such as basil, Italian parsley, and chives)

   Freshly cracked black pepper

2   tablespoons plain seltzer water or club soda

   Flaky sea salt for serving (optional)

Frittatas are one of my preferred ways to use up small bits kicking around in the fridge that need a career path. Be it a few green onions, a lone tomato, or a block of cheese, you can already be halfway to a meal with a few simple additions. The secret ingredient here is seltzer water, which may be new to you in a frittata. The bubbles give the frittata a bit of lightness and lift without the addition of lots of milk and cream. Eat it morning, noon, and night—it always satisfies.

1   Preheat the oven to 325°F.

2   In a 12-inch cast-iron or nonstick ovenproof skillet over medium heat, warm 1 tablespoon of the olive oil. Add the onion and sauté, stirring, for 3 to 5 minutes until translucent.

3   Add the mushrooms and cook for about 5 minutes until lightly browned.

4   Add the spinach with the salt, give it another stir, and cook until the spinach is just wilted before removing the mixture from the pan onto a plate.

5   Crack the eggs into a large bowl, add the milk and beat lightly with a fork. Add the Cheddar, herbs, and pepper to taste, and the seltzer, and stir only once. You don't want to disrupt the bubbles in the seltzer.

6   In the same skillet set over medium-high heat, heat the remaining 1 tablespoon of olive oil.

7   When hot, add the egg mixture and cook, stirring with a rubber spatula and scraping the bottom and sides until partially set, about 30 seconds. Add in the mushroom-spinach mixture, distributing it evenly in the frittata. Smooth the top with a spatula, then transfer to the oven to cook for 20 to 25 minutes until set.

8   Cool briefly in the pan before cutting into wedges and serving, topped with a sprinkling of flaky salt if using.

SUPERFOOD BLENDER PANCAKES

MAKES 12 TO 14 PANCAKES

1 cup old-fashioned rolled oats

2 large eggs

1 tablespoon creamy almond butter

1 ripe banana, mashed

½ cup frozen cauliflower rice, defrosted

½ cup gluten-free all-purpose flour

1 teaspoon baking powder

¼ teaspoon kosher salt

1 cup unsweetened almond milk

Coconut oil for frying

Cauliflower?! I know, I know. Before you seriously question my judgment, know that cauliflower has a neutral taste and will take on whatever flavors you put it with. Blend it up with loads of healthy fats, fiber, and protein and you've got a pancake that is tasty and virtuous at the same time. I always have a bag of frozen cauliflower rice in my freezer, in large part to make these kid-approved pancakes every Saturday morning. Oh, and if you're my husband reading this: Hello! You've been eating cauliflower in your pancakes too.

Freeze extra pancakes for a quick, healthy weekday breakfast. I find they reheat very well in the toaster oven.

1 In a large, high-powered blender, blend the oats for 10 to 20 seconds until they resemble flour. Add in the eggs, almond butter, banana, and cauliflower rice and blend again for 10 seconds.

2 Add the flour, baking powder, salt, and almond milk and blend again just until smooth. Let the batter rest for 5 minutes to thicken further.

3 Grease a large cast-iron skillet or griddle with coconut oil and set over medium-low heat. It's important that your heat isn't too high, or the pancakes will cook too quickly on the outside to give the insides time to set.

4 Pour scant ¼ cup portions onto the skillet, leaving a couple of inches in between each.

5 Cook for 2 to 4 minutes, until bubbles start to form on top, then flip and cook for another 2 to 4 minutes.

6 Continue in batches until all the batter is used up. If the batter starts to get too thick, mix in a bit more almond milk to loosen it.

7 Serve right away, with butter and maple syrup or berries and yogurt.

GOAT CHEESE FRIED EGGS

MAKES 2 TO 4 SERVINGS

2 teaspoons extra-virgin olive oil

2 ounces goat cheese, crumbled

4 large eggs

Kosher salt

Freshly cracked black pepper

2 tablespoons minced chives for serving

What's better than a classic fried egg? Goat Cheese Fried Eggs. These eggs take just minutes to make, and instead of using butter or oil, we use creamy, tangy goat cheese to supply the fat to cook the eggs. Don't fuss when the goat cheese browns and clumps up a bit around your eggs—it's these burnished, scraggly cheese bits that I love the most.

1 Heat a large nonstick frying pan over medium heat.

2 Once hot, add the olive oil and goat cheese to the pan and allow it to soften for one minute. When the goat cheese is soft and melting, crack the eggs into the pan on top of and alongside the cheese.

3 Sprinkle with a large pinch each of salt and pepper.

4 Cover with a lid and cook the eggs for 3 to 4 minutes or until the whites are set and no longer translucent and the cheesy bits have browned in the pan. To cook the tops of the eggs without flipping, place a tablespoon of water in the pan and cover with a lid for 2 minutes, allowing the water to steam the tops of the eggs.

5 Remove the eggs from the pan, placing one or two on each plate, sprinkle with chives, and serve immediately.

SKILLET BAKED APPLES *WITH* OAT GINGER CRUMBLE

MAKES 6 SERVINGS

¾   cup old-fashioned rolled oats

3   tablespoons almond flour

3   tablespoons coconut oil, melted

3   tablespoons maple syrup

½   teaspoon ground cinnamon

¼   teaspoon ground ginger

½   teaspoon kosher salt

3   large, firm sweet/tart apples
    (such as Pink Lady, Honeycrisp, or
    Jonagold)

Baked apples are one of those dishes that teeter on the line between breakfast and dessert, in my view, depending on how nutritious the preparation. We are essentially making a quick granola mixture here and laying it on apples that have been halved and cored, which allows them to cook quicker and more evenly than leaving them whole. The rule of thumb for baking apples is to use fruit that is firm enough not to leave an indent when pressed with your finger. I reach for Pink Lady apples most often for this recipe. This meal is a lovely and somewhat unexpected offering for an autumnal brunch when paired with your favorite yogurt. Leftovers, of course, can be dessert with ice cream.

1   Preheat the oven to 375°F.

2   In a small mixing bowl, combine the oats, almond flour, melted coconut oil, maple syrup, cinnamon, ginger, and salt. Mix with a spoon and set aside.

3   Cut each apple in half lengthwise and scoop out the seeds with a melon baller or small spoon. Slice off a very thin piece of apple skin from the rounded side to allow the apples to lay flat as they bake. Place them in a cast-iron pan or baking dish, seeded side up.

4   Distribute the oat crumble evenly on the apples, covering the tops completely to keep them moist.

5   Bake the apples for 35 to 40 minutes, depending on the size of the apples, until they are tender and the crumble is golden brown.

6   Serve with yogurt and another drizzle of maple syrup if you like.

BETTER FOR YOU GRANOLA

MAKES 6 CUPS

3 cups old-fashioned rolled oats

½ cup raw seeds (such as pumpkin and sunflower)

1 cup untoasted nuts (such as almonds, pecans, or walnuts, or a mixture of all three)

1 large egg white, lightly beaten

½ cup maple syrup

¼ cup coconut oil, melted

½ teaspoon vanilla extract

1 teaspoon kosher salt

½ teaspoon ground cinnamon

⅛ teaspoon ground cardamom

½ cup flaked unsweetened coconut

Granola is a sneaky character. It's essentially a deconstructed oatmeal raisin cookie parading around as a health food. I want to know who is doing granola's PR. But this granola is different, with a fraction of the fat and sugar you find in most varieties. The trick to still obtaining the crunchiest granola means relying on an unlikely ingredient: egg white. It does a bang-up job of binding the granola into beautiful clusters without using an excessive amount of oil. This is the only granola recipe I use these days, because I prefer to eat my cookies at nine p.m. in my robe, not with my morning coffee. This granola can be eaten as is, fruit-free, or with dried cherries, apricots, or chopped dark chocolate added after it has cooled.

1 Preheat the oven to 350°F and line a baking sheet with parchment paper.

2 In a large bowl, combine the oats, seeds, nuts, egg white, maple syrup, coconut oil, vanilla, salt, cinnamon, and cardamom.

3 Transfer the mixture to the baking sheet, patting it down flat to cover as much surface area as possible. This will encourage crispy granola.

4 Bake for 20 minutes, then add in the coconut and stir once. Bake for another 15 to 20 minutes until golden brown.

5 Set the baked granola aside to cool completely before breaking it up into large clusters. Store it in the refrigerator, covered, where it will keep for up to 1 month.

TURKEY SAUSAGE
WITH APPLE AND SAGE

MAKES 10 PATTIES

1 pound ground dark turkey meat, patted dry

½ cup finely diced Granny Smith apple

2 garlic cloves, minced

½ teaspoon dried sage

½ teaspoon paprika

¼ teaspoon ground fennel seed

1 teaspoon kosher salt

¼ teaspoon freshly cracked black pepper

1 tablespoon maple syrup

2 tablespoons extra-virgin olive oil, for pan-frying

We are a big poultry sausage family: turkey and chicken sausage are in heavy rotation around here, both in breakfast preparations like this one and in savory soups and skillets that you'll find later in the book. This is a nice side to serve to company, as it goes with almost any breakfast food you can think of, and feels unique. I like to bring the turkey to room temperature for an hour before using so it cooks more evenly. Do make sure you use ground dark turkey, as ground turkey breast is much too dry for this sausage (and most anything, really, but I digress).

You will cook these in two batches so you don't overcrowd the pan, which would keep them from forming a nice crust on the outside.

1 In a medium bowl, combine the ground turkey, diced apple, garlic, sage, paprika, fennel seed, salt, pepper, and maple syrup. Briefly and gently mix together with a large spoon or preferably your hands.

2 With wet hands, form 10 small, thin patties using ¼ cup of the meat mixture at a time.

3 Heat a large cast-iron skillet over medium-high heat and line a plate with a paper towel.

4 When the skillet is hot, add 1 tablespoon of the olive oil, and then after it is hot, half of the turkey patties. Cook for 3 to 5 minutes per side until the patties are well browned and no longer pink in the center. Keep an eye on them: overcooking will result in a dry turkey sausage.

5 Remove the patties to the prepared plate. Add the remaining 1 tablespoon of oil to the skillet and repeat for the second batch of turkey sausage.

6 Serve alone or with a drizzle of maple syrup on top, alongside eggs or French toast.

*

SNACKS

+

APPS

CRISPY AIR-FRIED ARTICHOKES WITH SIMPLE TOMATO SAUCE

MAKES 4 SERVINGS

2   (15-ounce) cans artichoke hearts in water, drained

2   garlic cloves, minced

2   tablespoons extra-virgin olive oil

    Kosher salt

    Freshly cracked black pepper

1   cup Simple Tomato Sauce (recipe follows) for serving

I don't even recall how I decided to air-fry a can of artichokes, but I remember what I was wearing the day that I did because the video went viral. I took a video of what seemed like it might be a decent idea, and after taking a bite and being a bit shocked at how delicious they were, I posted it to social media. Since then, the amount of people that have made these easy, inexpensive, crispy, garlicky artichokes is far more than I ever anticipated, but I'm also not surprised. They are the best thing you will do with a can of artichokes. Promise.

1   Using a paper towel, pat the artichokes dry really well. Removing the water will allow them to crisp up nicely as you air-fry, so be gentle and thorough.

2   In a medium bowl, combine the artichokes with the garlic, oil, a large pinch of salt, and a few cracks of pepper.

3   Transfer the mixture to the air-fryer and fry at 400°F for 15 minutes until the artichokes are crispy and browned. Serve on a platter with a small bowl of tomato sauce for dipping.

SIMPLE TOMATO SAUCE

Makes about 2½ cups

1   tablespoon extra-virgin olive oil

2   garlic cloves, minced

1   (28-ounce) can whole San Marzano tomatoes

¼   teaspoon kosher salt

⅛   teaspoon freshly cracked black pepper

In a medium pot, warm the oil over medium-low heat.

Add the garlic and cook, stirring, for 30 seconds until it just starts to brown. Stir in the tomatoes with their juices, and the salt and pepper.

Bring the sauce to a simmer and cook for about 30 minutes, until the tomatoes appear to be falling apart. Using a potato masher or heavy wooden spoon, mash the tomatoes so they fall apart a bit more. Remove the sauce from the heat and serve in a small bowl alongside the artichokes.

FETA-STUFFED OLIVES WITH ZA'ATAR

MAKES 30 STUFFED OLIVES

1	large lemon (organic if possible)
3	teaspoons za'atar
½	cup extra-virgin olive oil
3	tablespoons chopped fresh parsley
1	teaspoon red pepper flakes
¼	teaspoon kosher salt
¼	teaspoon freshly cracked black pepper
1	(2-ounce) block feta cheese, cut into small sticks
30	pitted, large Castelvetrano olives (about 8 ounces)

Shall we normalize practicing restraint with appetizers ahead of a big meal? I don't want my guests filling up so much they can't fully enjoy the main spread (but I am guilty of having been that guest myself). These olives are the perfect sort of bites to put out with cocktails: salty, creamy, and bright with lemon zest, herbs, and spices. Za'atar is a Middle Eastern spice that can be found at most large grocery stores nowadays, but if you can't track it down, throw in a few sprigs of fresh thyme or a tablespoon of coriander seeds instead. These will still be some of the best olives your guests have ever had.

1. Using a peeler, remove the lemon peel in large strips. Cut each lemon peel segment lengthwise into thin strips. Reserve the peeled lemon for another use.

2. Add to a medium bowl the lemon peel strips, za'atar, olive oil, parsley, red pepper flakes, salt, and pepper and stir together. Set aside.

3. Stuff a feta stick into each olive by using the wide end of a chopstick or your fingers. Add the stuffed olives to the za'atar mixture in the bowl, and toss to combine. Cover and chill for at least 4 hours or up to 3 days. Let the olives come to room temperature before serving.

FIVE-MINUTE TZATZIKI

MAKES 2½ CUPS

1   English cucumber, finely grated

½   teaspoon kosher salt

2   cups full-fat plain Greek yogurt

2   garlic cloves, grated

    Juice of ½ lemon

¼   cup finely chopped fresh dill

3   teaspoons extra-virgin olive oil

From Greece and Turkey to India, many countries have a version of this dip. In fact there is some controversy over whether or not this is a dip or a salad, since cucumber is one of the main ingredients here. Whatever you call it, it's creamy, refreshing, and packed with flavor from the thick yogurt, mashed garlic, lemon juice, and dill.

My husband, Michael, adores tzatziki and got me tucking into it with kettle-cooked potato chips, a dynamite combination that pairs as well with cocktail hour as it does with a movie on Netflix.

1   Place the grated cucumber in a colander and sprinkle with the salt. Toss with your hand to combine and leave it to sit in the sink for about 15 minutes.

2   Transfer the cucumber to a thin kitchen towel and squeeze to remove as much water as possible. This will ensure a thick and creamy tzatziki. Transfer the wilted cucumber to a bowl.

3   Add the yogurt, garlic, lemon juice, dill, and 2 teaspoons of the olive oil and stir to combine.

4   Drizzle with the remaining 1 teaspoon of the olive oil when serving. Serve with pita bread and crudites or potato chips.

5   Alternatively, store in a lidded container in the refrigerator for up to 1 week.

WINE BAR NUT MIX

MAKES 4 CUPS

4 cups raw mixed nuts (such as almonds, cashews, pecans, and walnuts)

2 tablespoons maple syrup

1 tablespoon extra-virgin olive oil

1 tablespoon minced fresh rosemary

1 tablespoon minced fresh thyme

⅛ teaspoon cayenne

2 teaspoons kosher salt

These spectacular mixed nuts have it all: a crunchy, caramel-like exterior that envelops the nuts in warm, salty-sweet deliciousness, and rosemary and thyme for herbaceous warmth and just a hint of spice. They will stay fresh in the fridge for up to a month, which means you can always have them on hand to serve with drinks. You can also bag them up with a ribbon for gifts at the holidays, when everyone is already swimming in cookies and will welcome something else. These will make you the most popular neighbor on the block.

1 Preheat the oven to 350°F.

2 In a bowl, toss the nuts with the maple syrup, olive oil, rosemary, thyme, cayenne, and salt. Spread the nuts on a rimmed baking sheet and bake for 15 to 20 minutes, stirring halfway through, until their coating is browned and dry. Remove from the oven and toss briefly to break them up. Let cool completely before serving.

3 Store for up to 1 week at room temperature or 1 month in the fridge.

FRENCH DEVILED EGGS

MAKES 12 EGG HALVES

6 large eggs

¼ cup mayonnaise

1 tablespoon cornichon brine

1 tablespoon fresh dill, plus more for serving

Zest of ½ lemon

2 tablespoons finely chopped cornichons

Flaky sea salt

Freshly cracked black pepper

Deviled eggs are always the first thing to be gobbled up at a barbecue, but they are not all created equally. While I love the classic American deviled egg, this recipe has a bit more cachet. Inspired by the French preparation, we're using the combination of dill, lemon, and cornichon, which adds such a bright flavor to the eggs and shows us that a beautiful plate of boiled eggs isn't only possible but easy, and they are delicious.

1 Prepare a large bowl of water with ice cubes to use for the cooked eggs.

2 Add 2 inches of water to a large pot. Cover and bring to a boil over high heat. Add eggs to the pot, lower the heat to simmer, and re-cover. Cook the eggs for 12 to 14 minutes for hard-boiled.

3 Upon removing the eggs from the pot, immediately place them in the bowl of ice water and allow them to cool for 3 minutes.

4 To peel, first gently roll the egg on a hard surface with your palm to thoroughly crack the shell, then place it back in the cold water while you roll the other eggs. This allows water to get under the shells. Remove the shells starting at the wide end (where the air pocket is) under a thin stream of running water.

5 Pat the eggs dry and cut in half lengthwise. Leave the yolks in the eggs.

6 In a small bowl, combine the mayonnaise, cornichon brine, 1 tablespoon of dill, and the lemon zest. Mix with a fork until well blended. Dollop the egg halves with the mayonnaise mixture and top each with the cornichons, a sprinkle of flaky salt, a few cracks of pepper, and more dill.

HERBED ZUCCHINI FRITTERS
WITH SALTED YOGURT

MAKES 6 TO 10 SERVINGS ✳ ABOUT 18 FRITTERS

3 to 4 medium zucchini, grated
(about 1 pound, or 6 cups)

½ small onion, grated (about ⅓ cup)

SALTED YOGURT

1 cup full-fat plain Greek yogurt

Juice and zest of ½ lemon

Kosher salt

1 teaspoon kosher salt

2 large eggs, lightly beaten

1 garlic clove, minced

1 tablespoon chopped fresh dill

1 tablespoon chopped fresh basil

Freshly cracked black pepper

⅓ cup gluten-free all-purpose flour

½ teaspoon baking powder

Zest of 1 lemon

Neutral oil for frying

Flaky sea salt for serving

We all know that when zucchini steps on stage it comes in *hot*. There is only so much zucchini you can roast, shave, and bake with before you start to tire of it. These fritters are a lovely way to use up that bounty: crispy on the outside and tender inside, with a cool yogurt dipping sauce. If you're swimming in zucchini, make a double or triple batch of these fritters and freeze them. You can reheat them in the oven or air-fryer to return them to golden, summery perfection. Don't skip the flaky salt at the end—fried foods need a dash of salt to make them sing.

1 Place the grated zucchini and onion in a colander over a bowl or sink and sprinkle with the salt. Let it sit for 10 minutes to drain before transferring it to a thin kitchen towel and squeezing over a bowl or sink to remove as much liquid as possible. You will have about 4 cups of vegetables now.

2 **TO MAKE THE SALTED YOGURT:** Whisk together the yogurt, lemon juice and zest, and a pinch of kosher salt in a medium bowl and refrigerate until ready to serve as a dipping sauce.

3 Whisk the eggs in a large bowl. Add the grated zucchini and onion, garlic, dill, basil, pepper to taste, flour, baking powder, and lemon zest. Mix with a rubber spatula to combine well.

4 Line a plate with a paper towel and set aside. Heat about 2 tablespoons of oil in a large cast-iron skillet over medium-high heat until hot. It should sizzle when a drop of water hits it.

5 Working in batches, drop 2-tablespoon portions of batter into the pan. Flatten each slightly with the back end of the spatula into a little pancake. The fritters should be nice and thin so they cook evenly. Cook, flipping once, until browned, 3 to 4 minutes on each side.

6 Transfer to the plate and sprinkle with flaky salt. Repeat with the remaining batter, adding 2 tablespoons of oil before each batch.

7 Serve immediately with the Salted Yogurt on the side for dipping.

8 Fritters can be reheated under a broiler for 1 or 2 minutes.

MARINATED GOAT CHEESE

MAKES 6 SERVINGS

1   teaspoon mixed red, black, and
     white peppercorns

½   teaspoon whole coriander seeds

2   bay leaves, broken into pieces
     Extra-virgin olive oil

6   ounces goat cheese (in a log)

3   sprigs thyme

This recipe is the definition of low effort, high reward. The goat cheese takes a quick bath in spiced herb-flecked olive oil to become a fancier version of itself in no time at all. I love to take a familiar ingredient like goat cheese and serve it in a new way so that guests at my table ask eager questions but are familiar enough with the ingredients to try it. If you don't have whole coriander seeds, simply add more peppercorns.

I like to use unflavored dental floss to slice goat cheese, but a sharp knife works too. If you find your knife isn't sharp enough, pop the log in the freezer for a few minutes to make it easier to slice.

This gussied-up goat cheese is a welcome addition to any cheese board, and it makes a great gift too.

1   Place the peppercorns and coriander seeds on a cutting board and smash them with the side of a knife. Transfer the smashed peppercorns and seeds along with the broken bay leaves to a clean, sterilized wide-mouthed jar with a lid. Pour in ¼ cup of the oil.

2   Cut the goat cheese into ½-inch-thick rounds. Place one round of cheese in the jar and drizzle on some olive oil. Stack the remaining rounds, drizzling oil onto each round before topping with the next. Add the thyme to the jar and pour in enough olive oil to cover the goat cheese rounds completely. Cover the jar and leave at room temperature for up to 3 hours before refrigerating. Serve in the jar with a knife for spreading, at room temperature with toasted bread and water crackers.

MOSTLY SPINACH DIP

MAKES 6 TO 8 SERVINGS ✳ 3 CUPS

2   tablespoons extra-virgin olive oil

1   medium onion, finely chopped
     (about 1½ cups)

4   garlic cloves, minced

1¼   teaspoons kosher salt

1   (16-ounce) package frozen
     whole-leaf spinach, defrosted,
     excess liquid squeezed out, and
     chopped

¾   cup full-fat plain Greek yogurt

¾   cup (6 ounces) reduced-fat cream
     cheese

½   cup shredded part-skim mozzarella

½   teaspoon freshly cracked black
     pepper

     Pinch of nutmeg

¼   cup freshly grated Parmesan
     cheese

There is something reliable about spinach dip that will lure people from all corners of the room to grab a chip and tuck into its cheesy, savory goodness. Ask yourself: Do you know anyone who doesn't like spinach dip? I don't.

Here we have dropped the traditional mayo and are using a combination of Greek yogurt and reduced-fat cream cheese as the base. We've also used some mozzarella and Parmesan for that trademark cheesiness. The pinch of nutmeg might sound odd, but trust me. Nutmeg is used in classic steakhouse creamed spinach for its ability to provide a subtle warmth to the inherently savory dish. It is that little something that brings it all home.

1   Preheat the oven to 375°F.

2   Heat 1 tablespoon of the oil in a sauté pan over medium-low heat. Add the onion and cook, stirring occasionally, for 4 to 5 minutes until lightly browned. Add the garlic and ¼ teaspoon of the salt and cook an additional 3 to 4 minutes, or until the onions are light golden but not browned. Remove from the heat, place on a plate, and let cool to room temperature.

3   Pat the spinach as dry as you can and place it in the bowl of a food processor. Add the yogurt, cream cheese, ¼ cup of the mozzarella, the remaining 1 teaspoon of salt, the pepper, and the nutmeg. Process until smooth.

4   Add the onion mixture to the food processor and pulse just 2 or 3 times to combine. Coat a broiler-safe baking dish (8-inch square or 10 by 7 inches) with the remaining 1 tablespoon of olive oil.

5   Transfer the spinach dip into the dish and top with the remaining ¼ cup of mozzarella and the Parmesan. Bake for 15 to 20 minutes, or until the dip is heated through and bubbling.

6   Turn the broiler to high and broil for 3 to 4 minutes until the top is well browned. Serve with pita wedges or crudites.

NOTE *If made ahead, refrigerate the dip for up to 24 hours and bake, covered, for 20 to 30 minutes at 350°F until warm and bubbling.*

PARTY SHRIMP BITES

MAKES 26 TO 30 SHRIMP BITES

1 tablespoon sriracha

½ teaspoon Worcestershire sauce

½ teaspoon honey

1 tablespoon extra-virgin olive oil

2 garlic cloves, finely minced

2 tablespoons finely minced fresh cilantro

1 teaspoon kosher salt

⅛ teaspoon freshly cracked black pepper

1 pound large shrimp, peeled and deveined

Juice of ½ lime

These shrimp bites are the perfect appetizer to serve for game day, especially if you're anything like me and believe that the best thing about a game day is the plentiful food. The bites carry a spicy punch, so if you're sensitive to heat, scale back on the sriracha. If you like *lots* of spice, double it. It's the trifecta of sriracha, Worcestershire, and honey that makes these shrimp so addictive. Serve a big pile of these guys with toothpicks and napkins and watch them disappear. The only real time commitment in this recipe is the 2 to 4 hours that the shrimp need to marinate in the fridge. Once that's done, they cook in minutes.

1 In a large bowl, mix together the sriracha, Worcestershire, honey, olive oil, garlic, 1 tablespoon of the cilantro, the salt, and the pepper. Add the shrimp to the marinade and toss to coat completely.

2 Marinate in the fridge for 2 to 4 hours.

3 In a 12-inch nonstick skillet set over medium heat, cook the shrimp in one layer, undisturbed, until they just turn pink, about 2 minutes. Flip and cook for 1 to 2 minutes more until cooked through, then remove the pan from the heat.

4 Pile the shrimp onto a shallow serving platter, top with the remaining 1 tablespoon of cilantro and the lime juice, and serve with toothpicks. They won't last long.

STUFFED MUSHROOMS WITH PROSCIUTTO BREAD CRUMBS

MAKES 6 TO 8 SERVINGS

20	to 24 large button or cremini mushrooms, washed
⅓	cup panko-style bread crumbs
⅓	cup freshly grated Parmesan cheese
3	ounces prosciutto, finely diced
½	cup finely diced fresh parsley, plus more for garnish
1	tablespoon chopped fresh sage leaves, chopped
2	garlic cloves, minced
	Kosher salt
	Freshly cracked black pepper
	Extra-virgin olive oil

Stuffed mushrooms have always been a favorite appetizer of mine. Growing up we reserved them for special holidays, like Christmas Day. I could smell the buttery bread crumbs and garlic baking from two rooms away. It was one of the only things that could get me to abandon staring at my gifts from that morning. Here I have a lighter take on the classic stuffed mushroom, keeping a moderate amount of cheese and olive oil and adding in more flavor from sage and prosciutto—the prosciutto makes for a pretty presentation, as well. These mushroom crowns flecked with red and green are the appetizer I'll serve for Christmas for a lifetime.

1   Preheat the oven to 400°F and line a large baking sheet with parchment paper.

2   Remove the stems from the mushrooms and slice off and discard just the exposed bottom of the stem. Coarsely chop the stems and add to a medium bowl.

3   Add the panko, Parmesan, prosciutto, parsley, sage leaves, garlic, a small pinch of salt, and several grinds of pepper. Drizzle in 1 tablespoon of the olive oil and mix to combine.

4   Place the mushrooms, cavity side up, on the baking sheet. Drizzle the mushrooms with olive oil and sprinkle with ¼ teaspoon of salt. Rub all over.

5   Spoon a generous amount of filling into the mushrooms. It's okay if it spills down the sides a bit. Just tuck as much as you can into the cavities.

6   Drizzle with a bit more olive oil, then bake until the mushrooms are tender and the filling is golden brown, 18 to 22 minutes. Serve right away.

HASSELBACK CAPRESE

MAKES 8 SERVINGS

8   large Roma tomatoes

2   (8-ounce) balls fresh mozzarella

16   fresh basil leaves

2   tablespoons extra-virgin olive oil

2   tablespoons One-Ingredient Balsamic Glaze (page 261) or store-bought balsamic glaze

   Flaky sea salt

   Freshly cracked black pepper

In the height of summer, there's not much better than a juicy, sweet tomato, is there? That's why when the temperatures climb I eat my weight in tomatoes any way I can for as many weeks as they will stick around. Here we take a classic summer combination—tomato, mozzarella, and basil—and we present it in a new way. It's just as delicious as you've ever had, and so much more fun to serve. I always get a few "Ohhhh, how cute!" comments, and I quite like that element of surprise.

1   Slice a thin piece off the stem end of the tomato and discard.

2   Slice a thin piece of flesh from the long side of the tomato so that it sits without wobbling about.

3   Using a serrated knife, evenly score the tomatoes crosswise, making 4 to 6 cuts, depending on the tomato's size. Slice three-quarters of the way down. Pay attention that you don't cut all the way through, but please don't stress. One way to do this as you're getting the hang of it is to use chopsticks on both sides of the tomato. This will stop the knife from going all the way through as you cut perpendicularly to them.

4   Slice the mozzarella balls in half, then place them cut-side down on your board and thinly slice them into half-moons.

5   Lay a small basil leaf on top of each piece of mozzarella cheese. If some leaves are large, cut them in half and use half at a time. Gently push a slice of cheese with its basil leaf into each cut in the tomato. The cheese should be flush with the top of the tomato. Repeat this process with the remaining tomatoes, mozzarella, and basil until all of the tomatoes have been stuffed.

6   Drizzle the olive oil and balsamic glaze all over the tomatoes and sprinkle generously with flaky salt and black pepper. Serve.

MEDJOOL DATES
WITH CITRUS, GOAT CHEESE, AND THYME

MAKES 10 SERVINGS ✳ 20 DATES

⅓   cup goat cheese, room temperature

1   teaspoon chopped fresh thyme

1   teaspoon orange zest

⅛   teaspoon kosher salt

20   large, plump Medjool dates

20   toasted pecans (about 1 cup)

No-cook appetizers are the ones I make and serve most often. Not only are they usually very quick to make, but they can often be done ahead, leaving me time to focus on the main parts of the meal on the day of. These little stuffed dates are no exception. Chewy, plump dates are filled with an herb-and-citrus-flecked goat cheese and topped with a toasted pecan, making for an inviting and stress-free way to start a party.

1   In a small bowl, mix together the goat cheese, thyme, orange zest, and salt with a spoon.

2   Using a sharp paring knife, make a slit down the side of each date and gently remove the pit. You want the date itself to stay intact.

3   Fill each date with about ½ teaspoon of the goat cheese mixture. Top each stuffed date with a toasted pecan and arrange them on a platter.

4   Serve right away or refrigerate for up to 2 days. If they were made ahead, bring the dates to room temperature by removing them from the fridge about 1 hour before serving.

BURRATA WITH ROASTED GRAPES

MAKES 4 SERVINGS

12 ounces seedless red grapes, on the vine

2 tablespoons red wine vinegar

2 tablespoons extra-virgin olive oil

Freshly cracked black pepper

3 sprigs rosemary, plus more for garnish

3 sprigs thyme, plus more for garnish

1 large ball burrata

Flaky sea salt

Toasted bread or crackers for serving

Burrata . . . we know her, we love her, but we think she can do better than a plate of greens and sliced tomato. Let's give her the treatment she deserves, shall we? This dish takes me back to living in Toronto in 2013, when Michael and I were dating and had no one's bedtimes to tend to but our own. We favored a cozy, rustic Italian restaurant called Campagnolo, eating there at least once a month, and I always ordered this appetizer. The grapes aren't even the wow factor here—it's how the method of roasting them makes them even sweeter. Their skins pop to release their crimson juices into the olive oil and herbs, providing you at once with just enough sauce to drizzle atop the creamy burrata. It's the closest we get to that cozy Italian restaurant in Toronto, and it feels special in a whole new way to eat these at our kitchen island in Connecticut.

1 Preheat the oven to 400°F.

2 In a large baking dish, gently toss the grapes with the red wine vinegar, olive oil, and a few cracks of pepper. Nestle the sprigs of rosemary and thyme under the grapes to allow them to perfume the grapes without burning.

3 Roast for about 30 minutes, until the grapes are blistered on the outside and have released some of their juices. There won't be much liquid.

4 Remove from the oven and discard the thyme and rosemary sprigs, reserving the juices and grapes in the pan. Let the grapes cool to room temperature.

5 Place the burrata on a large serving platter.

6 Arrange the grapes on the platter next to the burrata and drizzle them with the pan juices. Sprinkle the grapes and burrata generously with flaky salt and more cracked pepper and garnish with fresh rosemary and thyme sprigs to bring some color to the plate.

7 Serve with hearty toasted bread, letting each person top their bread with a smear of burrata and some grapes.

THE SILKIEST WHITE BEAN HUMMUS

MAKES 8 SERVINGS ✳ ABOUT 2 CUPS

2 (15-ounce cans) white beans, drained and rinsed

1 teaspoon baking soda

3 garlic cloves, halved and peeled

Juice of 1 to 2 lemons

½ cup tahini

1 to 2 teaspoons kosher salt

¼ cup extra-virgin olive oil

Optional toppings: ground cumin, paprika, cilantro, fresh chopped chives, or parsley

Slow-Roasted Tomatoes (page 264), optional

The day I learned to make hummus this way, my life changed.

I discovered this technique, boiling dried chickpeas with baking soda to break down the legume structure, in Yotam Ottolenghi's spectacular book *Jerusalem*. I wondered if doing the same with canned legumes could still result in sublimely smooth hummus in a fraction of the time. It does. With "hummus" translating to "chickpea" in Arabic, this is not traditional, as we are using mild, tender white beans instead. Consider this a gateway hummus recipe—it will convert even stubborn hummus skeptics. Just watch.

I like to top mine with a drizzle of olive oil, a little ground cumin and paprika, and fresh herbs such as cilantro, chives, or parsley. I also love to add Slow-Roasted Tomatoes (page 264) and their juices to the top of this one.

1 Place the white beans in a medium saucepan with the baking soda and garlic and cover with water. Bring to a boil, then lower the heat and simmer for 30 minutes.

2 Strain the beans and garlic and transfer the mixture to a high-speed blender. Juice one of the lemons into the blender.

3 Add the tahini, 1 teaspoon of the salt, and the olive oil.

4 Blend until smooth. This will take longer than you think: 1 to 2 minutes for silky smooth hummus, which is what we want.

5 If the hummus appears stiff and no longer blends easily, drizzle in a bit of ice water and blend until it reaches a silky enough consistency to sort of spill onto a plate.

6 Taste and add juice from the remaining lemon and another teaspoon of salt if desired.

7 In a shallow bowl, spread the hummus, making swirls with the back of a large spoon.

8 Serve with pita, veggies, chips, or crackers. Enjoy!

HUNGRY
LADY
SALADS

HUNGRY, HUNGRY LADIES LOVE
ENJOYING OUR FOOD . . .

I'M SORRY FOR YOU IF YOU
FIND IT RUDE.

IF WATCHING US PLEASURE OURSELVES
(DON'T LAUGH)

MAKES YOU FEEL SOMEWHAT AGHAST,

IT'S PROBABLY BEST THAT YOU
TAKE A COLD BATH.

WHEN PEOPLE SAY, "EAT LIKE
A LADY," WE ASK,

"WHY ARE THE LADIES ASSIGNED
THIS TASK?"

DON'T TALK WITH YOUR
MOUTH FULL,

DON'T MAKE A MESS . . .

BUT GROWN WOMEN DON'T MIND
A LITTLE SAUCE ON OUR DRESS.

IT'S NOT ABOUT MANNERS,
IT'S NOT ABOUT SIZE,

IT'S NOT ABOUT PLACING A
NAPKIN ON OUR THIGHS.

IT'S ABOUT EATING
WITH EXCITEMENT AND PRIDE

BECAUSE WE KNOW WE
DESERVE IT INSIDE.

SO IF WE SEE YOU EATING THE WAY
YOU SAY WE SHOULD,

WE KNOW WHAT YOU'RE EATING
JUST MUST NOT BE GOOD.

ROASTED CAULIFLOWER SALAD *WITH* SESAME DATE DRESSING

MAKES 6 TO 8 SERVINGS

1   large head cauliflower, cut into florets (about 8 cups)

1   (15-ounce) can chickpeas, drained

2   tablespoons extra-virgin olive oil

2   garlic cloves, minced

2   teaspoons za'atar

1   teaspoon kosher salt

¼   teaspoon freshly cracked black pepper

6   cups (5 ounces) mixed baby greens

1   large shallot, minced

3   celery stalks, diced

¼   cup chopped fresh parsley

¼   cup toasted sesame seeds

SESAME DATE DRESSING

4   dates, pitted

1   tablespoon whole-grain mustard

¼   cup tahini

¼   cup apple cider vinegar

¼   teaspoon kosher salt

¼   cup extra-virgin olive oil

⅓   cup cold water

In the colder months, I sometimes crave a warming salad, and I know many of you do too (judging by the many requests I've gotten for certain types of recipes). Here roasted cauliflower and chickpeas are tossed with a flavorful oil flecked with za'atar (because you bought it to make the Feta-Stuffed Olives with Za'atar [page 51], didn't you?). If you can't find za'atar, you can make your own by combining equal parts of cumin, thyme, sumac, and sesame. The combination really brightens up this toasty roasted salad.

1   Preheat the oven to 425°F.

2   On two large rimmed baking sheets, evenly divide the cauliflower, chickpeas, olive oil, garlic, za'atar, salt, and pepper. Toss to coat everything well. Transfer to the oven and roast for 20 minutes, rotating the pans between the racks halfway through, or until the cauliflower is tender and lightly charred.

3   Meanwhile, in a large salad bowl, combine the mixed baby greens, shallot, celery, parsley, and sesame seeds.

4   **TO MAKE THE SESAME DATE DRESSING:** In a high-speed blender, combine the dates, mustard, tahini, apple cider vinegar, salt, olive oil, and water. Blend for 10 seconds until smooth, scraping down the sides as needed.

5   Toss the room-temperature roasted cauliflower and chickpeas in with the salad. Add the vinaigrette and toss to coat if serving right away, or store separately for later. The undressed salad will keep for 3 to 5 days in the refrigerator.

BARBECUE RANCH CHOPPED SALAD

MAKES 6 TO 8 SERVINGS

DAIRY-FREE RANCH DRESSING

½ cup unsweetened plain coconut yogurt

½ cup mayonnaise

2 tablespoons white wine vinegar

1 teaspoon onion powder

1 teaspoon garlic powder

½ teaspoon dried dill

2 teaspoons dried parsley

2 teaspoons dried chives

1 teaspoon kosher salt

Freshly cracked black pepper

CHOPPED SALAD

2 (15-ounce) cans pinto beans, drained and rinsed

½ cup low-sugar barbecue sauce

¼ teaspoon kosher salt

6 romaine hearts (about 2 pounds), chopped into bite-size pieces

2 large ripe tomatoes, chopped

1 English cucumber, chopped

2 large, ripe avocados, chopped into 1-inch pieces

2 bunches green onions, white and green parts, sliced thin

2 large carrots, peeled and chopped

2 cups crumbled tortilla chips

The dairy-free ranch dressing we use here is reason alone to make this delicious salad. You will use it over and over again, in many ways. Feel free to add chicken if you're after the traditional barbecue chicken thing. This salad is chock-full of texture and color but it does play well with others.

1 **TO MAKE THE DAIRY-FREE RANCH DRESSING:** In a small bowl, combine the coconut yogurt, mayonnaise, vinegar, onion powder, garlic powder, dill, parsley, chives, salt, and a few cracks of pepper and whisk until very smooth. Reserve.

2 **TO MAKE THE CHOPPED SALAD:** In a medium saucepan pan over medium-low heat, combine the pinto beans with the barbecue sauce and salt. Cook for 1 to 2 minutes until warmed through, then set aside.

3 Place the chopped romaine in a large serving bowl.

4 Add in the tomatoes, cucumber, avocado, half of the green onions, and the carrots. Toss to combine. Drizzle in the dressing and toss to coat.

5 Top with the prepared barbecue beans, the tortilla chips, and the remaining green onions. Serve immediately.

BLT WEDGE SALAD WITH CROUTONS AND CREAMY BASIL DRESSING

MAKES 4 SERVINGS

CROUTONS

4	thick pieces hearty bread, a few days old
2	tablespoons extra-virgin olive oil
1	teaspoon kosher salt
½	teaspoon freshly cracked black pepper
3	to 4 slices bacon

CREAMY BASIL DRESSING

1	cup fresh basil leaves
1	large garlic clove, chopped
½	teaspoon kosher salt
¼	cup mayonnaise
2	tablespoons red wine vinegar
½	teaspoon Dijon mustard
2	tablespoons extra-virgin olive oil
1	large or two small tomatoes
1	large head iceberg lettuce
1	small red onion, thinly sliced
2	tablespoons finely minced chives
	Freshly cracked black pepper

Bacon, lettuce, tomato, and mayonnaise are a classic combination. You could call this salad a deconstructed BLT, and it has all the flavors and textures you're craving from one. You could go the steakhouse menu route and serve this as a starter with a steak dinner, or prep the ingredients and compose the salad for lunch during the week. If you've never made your own croutons before, you'll love how simple it is.

1. **TO MAKE THE CROUTONS:** Preheat the oven to 400°F. Line two baking sheets with parchment paper.

2. Cut the bread into ½-inch cubes. Transfer to one of the baking sheets and drizzle with the olive oil, salt, and pepper. Using your hands, gently toss the croutons, making sure they are coated with all the oil and seasonings, then spread them out evenly in the pan.

3. Lay the bacon on the second baking sheet.

4. Put both sheets into the oven at the same time, and line a plate with paper towels. Bake the croutons for 10 to 12 minutes until they are crunchy and golden brown. Bake the bacon for about 20 minutes, or until it is cooked to your liking.

5. **TO MAKE THE CREAMY BASIL DRESSING:** While the croutons and bacon are baking, in a blender combine the basil, garlic, salt, mayonnaise, red wine vinegar, mustard, and olive oil and blend for 10 to 15 seconds until smooth. Set aside.

6. Once the bacon is removed from the oven, allow it to cool slightly on the baking sheet. Remove to the prepared plate to cool completely. Crumble into pieces and set aside.

7. Halve the tomato and scoop out and discard the seeds. Dice into ½-inch pieces. Discard the outer leaves of the iceberg lettuce and cut into fourths through the core so that each quarter holds together.

8. Set each iceberg wedge on a plate and spoon the dressing over the top. Dress with the onion, tomatoes, bacon, and croutons, and garnish with the chives. Top each wedge with a couple of cracks of black pepper and serve.

LEMONY SWISS CHARD SALAD WITH WHITE BEANS AND GARLIC BREAD CRUMBS

MAKES 4 SERVINGS

Extra-virgin olive oil

1 cup Fresh Bread Crumbs (see page 260)

1 garlic clove, minced

Kosher salt

Red pepper flakes

1 lemon

¼ teaspoon Dijon mustard

1 large bunch Swiss chard (about 12 ounces)

1 (15-ounce) can white beans, drained, rinsed, and patted dry

1 shallot, thinly sliced

Many of you will know Swiss chard as a sturdy cold-weather green that is sautéed, but let's expand on that. Swiss chard makes a wonderful addition to or base of a salad, because it's both tender and sturdy, meaning it holds up well to weighty additions like white beans and a robust, lemony dressing. The soft bitterness of the chard combined with the creamy bellies of the beans and the crunchy bread crumbs makes for one lively bite of salad.

1 Warm 2 tablespoons of olive oil in a small, heavy skillet over medium heat. Add the bread crumbs and cook, stirring frequently, until they are crisp and golden brown, 4 to 6 minutes. Stir in the garlic, a pinch each of salt and red pepper flakes, and let toast for 30 seconds, then remove from the heat. Set aside.

2 In a large serving bowl, zest and juice the lemon.

3 Add the mustard and ¼ teaspoon of salt. Slowly whisk in ¼ cup of olive oil.

4 Wash and dry the chard and remove the stems from the leaves. Discard the stems or freeze them to make a pasta sauce or frittata someday.

5 Stack a few of the leaves on top of each other and roll them into a cigar shape. Slice the cigar crosswise into thin ribbons. Repeat with all of the leaves, then place them into the bowl with the dressing.

6 Toss the chard and dressing to coat.

7 Top with the white beans and shallot, then the bread crumbs. Serve.

MEDITERRANEAN CHOPPED SALAD *WITH* ROASTED RED PEPPER DRESSING

MAKES 6 TO 8 SERVINGS

ROASTED RED PEPPER DRESSING

1 (12-ounce) jar roasted red peppers, drained

1 large or 2 small garlic cloves, smashed

1 teaspoon honey

¼ cup balsamic vinegar

⅓ cup extra-virgin olive oil

Pinch of kosher salt

Pinch of freshly cracked black pepper

SALAD

2 romaine hearts, chopped

2 cups chopped cabbage

1 medium red onion, diced

2 cups cherry tomatoes, halved

1 cup green olives, pitted and sliced (preferably Castelvetrano)

1 (8-ounce) ball fresh mozzarella, diced

1 (15-ounce) can chickpeas, rinsed

Freshly cracked black pepper

I once received a message on social media from a woman in New Zealand who had gotten her sixty-five-year-old father into salad. She said he was making this salad and dressing to take on a fishing trip with his buddies that weekend. Picturing a group of burly sixty-something fishermen sharing a Hungry Lady Salad around a picnic table still makes me smile. This salad is one that transcends all genders, ages, and continents. It's universally delicious.

1 **TO MAKE THE ROASTED RED PEPPER DRESSING:** In a high-speed blender, combine the red peppers, garlic, honey, balsamic vinegar, olive oil, salt, and pepper. Blend for 20 to 30 seconds until very smooth, scraping down the blender as needed to incorporate. The dressing will look brown at first, then turns a bright orange-red as the peppers liquefy. Set aside.

2 **TO MAKE THE SALAD:** Combine the romaine, cabbage, onion, tomatoes, olives, mozzarella, and chickpeas in a large serving bowl and then drizzle with the dressing. Toss, finish with a few cracks of pepper, and serve.

ROASTED SWEET POTATO SALAD WITH SPICY CASHEW HERB DRESSING

MAKES 6 SERVINGS

2   pounds curly kale (about 2 generous bunches)

Kosher salt

2   large sweet potatoes, peeled and diced into 1-inch pieces

1   tablespoon extra-virgin olive oil

¼   teaspoon freshly cracked black pepper

SPICY CASHEW HERB DRESSING

1   garlic clove, smashed

1   teaspoon honey

½   teaspoon red pepper flakes

1   small bunch parsley

1   small bunch cilantro

¼   cup unsalted roasted cashews

⅓   cup unseasoned rice vinegar

½   cup extra-virgin olive oil

1   large avocado

3   green onions, white and green parts sliced thin

⅓   cup unsalted roasted cashews, chopped

I co-hosted an event with a local fitness studio and brought salads for all the guests to eat after class. In choosing which recipe to make, I knew I wanted a salad that (1) had no meat, gluten, or dairy, so it could be enjoyed no matter the guests' dietary restrictions; (2) was a tried-and-true recipe I knew people were already crazy about; (3) was filling and hearty enough to replenish their bodies after a good workout; and (4) was insanely delicious. The salad was a huge hit, and I'm still receiving messages about it.

1   Preheat the oven to 425°F.

2   Rinse, dry, and chop the kale, discarding the tough stems.

3   Add the kale to a large serving bowl and top with ¾ teaspoon of salt. Don't worry if it's overflowing in the bowl; it will shrink down as it softens. Using your hands, massage the salt into the kale for 10 to 20 seconds to soften it. Let it sit while you carry on.

4   On a large baking sheet, mix the sweet potatoes with the olive oil, ½ teaspoon of salt, and the black pepper. Spread in an even layer and roast for 15 to 20 minutes until browned and tender.

5   **TO MAKE THE SPICY CASHEW HERB DRESSING:** While the sweet potatoes are roasting, to a high-powered blender add the garlic, honey, pepper flakes, parsley, cilantro, cashews, rice vinegar, and olive oil and blend for 10 to 20 seconds, just until smooth and vibrant green. If you overblend, the dressing will become too thick. In that case, just add a tablespoon or two of water and pulse quickly to thin it out. Set aside.

6   Peel the avocado and dice into 1-inch cubes. To the bowl of kale, add the sweet potatoes, avocado, green onions, and chopped cashews. Drizzle with the dressing and toss gently and well.

7   Serve immediately, or store in the refrigerator for 3 to 5 days.

SOURDOUGH PANZANELLA WITH GOAT CHEESE AND PEACHES

MAKES 6 SERVINGS

3 cups cubed sourdough bread, preferably stale

6 tablespoons extra-virgin olive oil

Kosher salt

Freshly cracked black pepper

2 ripe peaches

2 pounds very ripe tomatoes

2 shallots, thinly sliced

¼ cup chopped fresh mint

¼ cup chopped fresh basil

4 tablespoons red wine vinegar

4 ounces crumbled goat cheese

Panzanella is a peasant Tuscan dish meant to use up leftover stale bread and overripe tomatoes—the dried bread soaks up the flavors of the vinaigrette and gets a lovely chew to it. I've taken this concept and added peaches, since I've always loved the combination of luscious peaches with acidic tomatoes, and the addition adds a pleasant sweetness to this traditionally savory salad. Be sure to dry the bread by baking completely so it doesn't get mushy and to let it rest in the refrigerator as directed. Both steps are necessary to let the flavors soak into the bread.

1 Preheat the oven to 425°F.

2 Spread the bread cubes on a rimmed baking sheet and toss with 2 tablespoons of the oil, ¼ teaspoon of salt, and a few cracks of pepper. Bake the bread cubes until they are dried out and pale golden brown at the edges, 10 to 15 minutes. Transfer the bread to cool on a wire rack while you make the salad.

3 Cut the peaches and tomatoes into wedges and place in a large serving bowl. Add the shallots, mint, basil, red wine vinegar, the remaining 4 tablespoons of olive oil, ¼ teaspoon of salt, and a few cracks of pepper. Toss gently.

4 Add the cooled bread cubes and goat cheese and toss gently once more to combine. Taste and add more salt if needed.

5 Refrigerate for at least 30 minutes and up to 4 hours before serving.

SUMMER CORN SALAD WITH AVOCADO

MAKES 6 SERVINGS

Kosher salt

6 ears of corn

3 cups cherry tomatoes, halved

1 English cucumber, diced

1 small red onion, sliced thin

2 small, ripe avocados

2 limes

1 tablespoon red wine vinegar

2 tablespoons extra-virgin olive oil

Freshly cracked black pepper

½ cup chopped fresh basil

¼ cup chopped fresh cilantro

This is a main character corn salad—nothing beats fresh corn, and this simple preparation doesn't provide distractions from its sweet, creamy taste. This salad is great for a cookout or potluck and goes with everything from grilled meats and fish to pizza. The sweetness of the corn is balanced by creamy avocado, bright tomatoes, and the freshness of herbs and lime. It's the perfect example of "simple is best."

1 Set a large stockpot full of generously salted water over medium-high heat and bring to a boil.

2 Shuck the cobs of their husks and add them to the boiling water.

3 Cook for just 2 to 3 minutes until bright yellow in color. Peak-season corn doesn't need long to cook, and you want to preserve the fresh flavor.

4 Place the corn cobs in a large serving bowl to cool. Once cool enough to handle, cut the kernels off the cobs into the bowl. Add the tomatoes, cucumber, and onion. Dice the avocado and put it on top.

5 Zest the limes directly over the vegetables, then squeeze the juice over the avocado. Add the red wine vinegar, olive oil, a generous pinch of salt, a few cracks of pepper, and the basil and cilantro.

6 Mix gently to combine. Taste, add salt if needed, and serve, or refrigerate for up to 2 days. (If you do refrigerate, first bury the avocado pieces in the salad to keep them protected from air, which would turn them brown. We like our avocado green.)

LENTIL CHOPPED SALAD WITH FETA AND HONEY WALNUT DRESSING

MAKES 6 TO 8 SERVINGS

Kosher salt

2   cups dried green lentils

HONEY WALNUT DRESSING

⅓   cup toasted walnuts

1   large garlic clove, smashed and peeled

1   tablespoon honey

⅓   cup apple cider vinegar

⅓   cup extra-virgin olive oil

½   teaspoon kosher salt

¼   teaspoon freshly cracked pepper

½   small head green cabbage, chopped fine (about 2 cups)

2   cups cherry tomatoes, halved

3   green onions, white and green parts, sliced thin

⅔   cup crumbled feta cheese

I don't know about you, but most lentil salads I've had just taste like . . . lentils. After two or three bites, I'm like, "Yeah, okay, I get it." This lentil salad is a whole lot more than just lentils.

Lentils play really well with others here, with lots of salty, creamy, crunchy additions from cabbage and tomatoes to feta cheese. The dressing gives a touch of rich sweetness that rounds the whole thing out. Is it the most beautiful salad? No, it's not. It's under the ugly-delicious category, and I'd eat it with pleasure no matter what it looked like.

1   Bring a medium saucepan of heavily salted water to a boil over medium-high heat. Rinse the dried lentils in a strainer, then add to the boiling water.

2   Cook for 15 to 20 minutes until the lentils are just tender but not falling apart.

3   **TO MAKE THE HONEY WALNUT DRESSING:** While the lentils cook, to a high-speed blender add the walnuts, garlic, honey, apple cider vinegar, olive oil, salt, and pepper and blend for about 20 seconds until smooth and thickened, with a bit of texture from the walnuts still at play. Set aside.

4   When the lentils are cooked, strain and rinse with cool water to bring them to room temperature. Add to a large serving bowl with the cabbage, tomatoes, green onions, and feta.

5   Toss gently to combine.

6   Drizzle the dressing over the salad and again toss gently until evenly coated. Serve immediately, or refrigerate for 4 to 5 days.

TEX-MEX COLESLAW WITH SMOKY LIME CREMA DRESSING

MAKES 6 TO 8 SERVINGS

SMOKY LIME CREMA DRESSING

- ⅓ cup mayonnaise
- ⅓ cup full-fat plain yogurt
- Juice of 3 limes
- ½ teaspoon ground cumin
- ½ teaspoon smoked paprika
- ½ teaspoon chili powder
- ½ teaspoon kosher salt
- ¼ teaspoon freshly cracked black pepper

COLESLAW

- 1 tablespoon extra-virgin olive oil
- 4 ears of corn, kernels removed
- Kosher salt
- 6 cups shredded red cabbage (about ½ medium cabbage)
- 2 small red peppers, thinly sliced
- 1 (15.25-ounce) can black beans, drained and rinsed
- 1 jalapeño, seeded and minced
- ½ cup chopped fresh cilantro
- 3 green onions, white and green parts sliced thin

I love coleslaw. There, I said it.

It gets judged by its worst representations, usually the slaw packed and preserved in the deli case for who knows how long. This coleslaw is fresh and crunchy, with sweetness from the corn and peppers, a bit of spice from the jalapeño, and a tart, creamy dressing with lime and smoked paprika. This slaw is ideal for any summer barbecue or make-ahead lunch when corn is at its peak, and will make you view coleslaw in a much more exciting light.

1 TO MAKE THE SMOKY LIME CREMA DRESSING: In a 16-ounce glass jar or small bowl, combine the mayonnaise, yogurt, lime juice, cumin, smoked paprika, chili powder, salt, and pepper and set aside to allow the flavors to marry while you prep the salad.

2 TO MAKE THE COLESLAW: In a skillet over medium-high, heat the olive oil. Add the corn with ¼ teaspoon of salt and cook until the kernels begin to char but are still crisp, 3 to 5 minutes. Set aside to cool slightly.

3 In large serving bowl, add the cabbage, red peppers, black beans, jalapeño, and ¼ cup of the cilantro. Add a big pinch of salt and stir in the green onions with the dressing.

4 Top with the remaining ¼ cup cilantro, cover, and refrigerate for 30 minutes before serving.

TUNA SALAD CHIP DIP

MAKES 4 TO 6 SERVINGS

DRESSING

- 1   tablespoon Dijon mustard
- 2   tablespoons pepperoncini brine
- 2   tablespoons red wine vinegar
- ¼   cup extra-virgin olive oil
     Pinch of kosher salt
     Pinch of freshly cracked black pepper

TUNA SALAD

- 4   (6-ounce) cans high-quality tuna in oil (I like Genova)
- ½   small red onion, finely diced
- 3   celery stalks, finely diced
- 6   pepperoncini, minced
- 2   tablespoons capers
- ⅓   cup minced fresh parsley
     Kosher salt
     Freshly cracked black pepper

You may know that a fork is the third most common utensil you'll see me eat a salad with. A big spoon is first, and a scoopable, edible medium like a chip or cracker is second. This tuna salad is a great alternative to the mayo tuna salads you may be used to (though I quite like those too). You'll need a jar of pepperoncini, and both the peppers and their brine add a ton of flavor, supplying both acid and brightness to a recipe that can sometimes be a bit bland. Use lots of salt and pepper, and grab a nice sturdy chip. You'll want big bites of this one for sure.

1   **TO MAKE THE DRESSING:** In a large bowl, combine the mustard, pepperoncini brine, red wine vinegar, olive oil, salt, and pepper and whisk until smooth.

2   **TO MAKE THE TUNA SALAD:** Drain the tuna well and add it to the bowl with the dressing.

3   Add the onion, celery, pepperoncini, capers, parsley, ½ teaspoon of salt, and ¼ teaspoon of pepper. Mix together until well combined. Taste. It should be highly seasoned—that is important in a tuna salad. Add more salt and pepper to taste.

4   Serve with tortilla chips or crackers. Leftovers will keep in the refrigerator for up to 1 week.

WARM ORZO SALAD WITH BALSAMIC MUSHROOMS

MAKES 4 TO 6 SERVINGS

Kosher salt

1½ cups dried orzo

Extra-virgin olive oil

8 ounces button mushrooms, sliced

Freshly cracked black pepper

4 tablespoons balsamic vinegar, plus more for finishing

5 ounces arugula

2 ounces watercress

½ small red onion, sliced thin

1 tablespoon chopped fresh tarragon

2 tablespoons chopped fresh parsley

½ cup grated fontina cheese

Juice of ½ lemon

½ cup chopped toasted walnuts

I'm crazy about mushrooms, and their deep, earthy flavor and meaty texture make them a great substitute for meat in vegetarian recipes like this one. The key to liking mushrooms, in my experience, is to cook them properly so they caramelize: Use a nice glug of cooking fat, don't overcrowd the pan, and salt at the end, since salt draws out moisture and mushrooms are full of it. The balsamic vinegar acts as a coating to encourage even further burnished flavor. Meat-eaters and vegetarians alike will be happy to have a big pile of this salad on their plate.

1 Bring a medium saucepan of salted water to a boil over medium-high heat. Cook the orzo until just tender according to package instructions.

2 Meanwhile, in a large skillet over medium heat, heat 2 tablespoons of olive oil. Add the mushrooms and sauté until lightly browned, about 5 minutes, stirring occasionally.

3 Add ½ teaspoon of salt, a few cracks of pepper, and 2 tablespoons of the balsamic. Stir just until the balsamic is absorbed, 15 to 20 seconds. Set aside.

4 In a large serving bowl, combine the arugula, watercress, red onion, tarragon, and parsley. Add the fontina, cooked orzo, and the balsamic mushrooms. Drizzle on 3 tablespoons of olive oil, the remaining 2 tablespoons of balsamic vinegar, the lemon juice, and ¼ teaspoon each of salt and pepper.

5 Toss to combine, then add the walnuts and toss again. Taste, and if it seems bland to you, add a bit more balsamic, olive oil, and salt to taste. Serve.

6 The salad will keep in the refrigerator, undressed, for up to 3 days.

GREEK QUINOA SALAD

MAKES 6 SERVINGS

Kosher salt

1 cup uncooked quinoa, rinsed

DRESSING

¼ cup extra-virgin olive oil

1 tablespoon red wine vinegar

Juice of ½ lemon

1 garlic clove, minced

½ teaspoon Dijon mustard

1 tablespoon minced fresh oregano (or 1 teaspoon dried)

3 cups grape tomatoes, halved

1 English cucumber, chopped

⅓ cup pitted kalamata olives, halved

⅓ cup minced red onion

½ cup crumbled Greek or Bulgarian feta cheese

¼ cup chopped fresh parsley

Freshly cracked black pepper

1 (6-ounce) bag mixed spring salad greens (baby spinach, arugula, or a combination)

Greek salad is always an easy sell. It's got that wonderful, refreshing briny flavor profile that keeps you coming back for more. When I'm at a diner with my kids (the height of fine dining with a four-year-old and a six-year-old) and don't know what I want to eat, a Greek salad is my go-to. One thing it always promises is bright, puckery flavor. Here we are adding quinoa and a traditional Greek dressing to make it a full meal in a bowl. Just the way we like it.

1 Bring a medium saucepan of heavily salted water to a boil over medium-high heat.

2 Cook the quinoa for 10 to 13 minutes until the quinoa is just tender. We are cooking this like pasta, so don't worry about the water-to-quinoa ratio.

3 **TO MAKE THE DRESSING:** While the quinoa is cooking, in a large bowl, whisk together the olive oil, red wine vinegar, lemon juice, garlic, mustard, and oregano. Set aside.

4 Drain the quinoa and put it back in the pot. Cover the top of the pot with a paper towel and put the lid back on. Allow the quinoa to sit for 5 to 7 minutes, then fluff with a fork.

5 Dump the quinoa into the bowl with the dressing along with the tomatoes, cucumber, olives, red onion, feta, and parsley. Toss well to combine. Taste, and add salt and pepper as needed.

6 Right before serving, add the salad greens to a large serving bowl. Add the quinoa mixture, toss, and serve. This salad will keep for up to 3 days in the refrigerator.

SHAVED CAESAR SALAD WITH FENNEL AND CRISPY CHICKPEAS

MAKES 4 SERVINGS

CRISPY CHICKPEAS

1	(15-ounce) can chickpeas, drained
1	tablespoon extra-virgin olive oil
½	teaspoon kosher salt

CAESAR DRESSING

3	oil-packed anchovy fillets, or 1 teaspoon anchovy paste
1	large garlic clove, smashed
¾	teaspoon kosher salt
¼	teaspoon freshly cracked black pepper
¼	cup mayonnaise
3	tablespoons lemon juice (1 lemon)
¾	teaspoon Dijon mustard
¼	cup neutral oil
3	tablespoons freshly grated Parmesan cheese

SALAD

1	large head romaine, thinly sliced into ribbons
1	large fennel bulb, sliced thin, fronds reserved for serving
1	small red onion, sliced thin
¼	cup finely grated fresh Parmesan cheese
	Freshly cracked black pepper

Caesar salad is one of my absolute favorite salads. Nothing beats that dressing—it's as perfect as can be. Some, though, balk at the raw egg, which we are replacing with mayonnaise here. This salad is absolutely crave-worthy, with an abundance of greens to welcome that glorious dressing, as well as crispy chickpeas and salty cheese to top it off. Don't skimp on the black pepper—it should be loud.

1 Preheat the oven to 450°F.

2 **TO MAKE THE CRISPY CHICKPEAS:** Pat the drained chickpeas *very* dry with paper towels to ensure they crisp up in the oven. Mix the chickpeas, olive oil, and salt on a large baking sheet and bake for about 20 minutes until crispy, shaking the pan halfway through. Set aside.

3 **TO MAKE THE CAESAR DRESSING:** While the chickpeas are baking, in a small blender or food processor, combine the anchovies, garlic, salt, pepper, mayonnaise, lemon juice, mustard, neutral oil, and Parmesan. Process for 10 seconds, or until smooth.

4 **TO MAKE THE SALAD:** In a large serving bowl, combine the romaine, sliced fennel bulb, and red onion. Drizzle with the salad dressing and toss to combine.

5 Top with the crispy chickpeas, fennel fronds, Parmesan, and a few cracks of pepper, and serve.

CHICKEN SALAD
WITH WALNUTS, APPLE,
AND TARRAGON

MAKES 8 TO 10 SERVINGS

2   pounds bone-in or boneless chicken breasts

Extra-virgin olive oil

Kosher salt

Freshly cracked black pepper

½   cup mayonnaise

⅓   cup full-fat plain Greek yogurt

1   tablespoon whole-grain mustard

3   tablespoons chopped fresh tarragon

1   small red onion, diced small

4   celery stalks, diced small

1   medium Granny Smith apple, diced small

½   cup chopped toasted walnuts

I couldn't let this chapter go without a recipe for a chicken salad. It's one lunch around here that everyone loves, and with two fickle small kids in the mix, that is no small feat. Think of a very good deli chicken salad, perfectly seasoned, with just the right amount of creaminess to hold it together, and lots of crunch. Then add tarragon, because chicken and tarragon are a delightful combination, and toasty walnuts for even more buttery crunch. That is what you'll have waiting for you for lunches all week long.

I use bone-in chicken breasts because they cook up juicier than boneless, but feel free to use boneless and cook at the low end of the time allotment if that's what you have.

1   Preheat the oven to 350°F.

2   Place the chicken breasts on a baking sheet and rub them with olive oil. Sprinkle generously with salt and pepper. Roast for 25 to 35 minutes until the chicken is cooked through. Set aside until cool.

3   In a large bowl, whisk together the mayonnaise, Greek yogurt, mustard, and tarragon. Add the red onion, celery, apple, and walnuts to the bowl.

4   When the chicken is cool, shred it with two forks, or cut it into a ¾-inch dice if that's the texture you prefer. Add it to the bowl and toss until the mayonnaise mixture is well incorporated.

5   Taste, and add salt if needed. The salad should be well seasoned.

6   Serve right away. Leftovers can be stored covered in the refrigerator for up to 5 days.

FALL FARMSTAND SALAD WITH FIG VINAIGRETTE

MAKES 6 SERVINGS

1 (2½- to 3-pound) butternut squash, peeled, seeds removed, and cut into ¾-inch dice (about 7 cups)

1 tablespoon extra-virgin olive oil

6 sprigs thyme

¼ teaspoon ground nutmeg

½ teaspoon kosher salt

⅛ teaspoon freshly cracked black pepper

SALAD

6 cups curly kale, stemmed and cut into bite-size pieces

3 cups shredded brussels sprouts

1 teaspoon kosher salt

FIG VINAIGRETTE

1 garlic clove, minced

Juice of ½ lemon

¼ cup apple cider vinegar

1 teaspoon Dijon mustard

2 tablespoons fig jam

½ teaspoon kosher salt

¼ teaspoon freshly cracked black pepper

½ cup extra-virgin olive oil

½ red onion, chopped

1 large crisp, tart apple (such as Granny Smith or Pink Lady), cubed

⅔ cup toasted pumpkin seeds

⅔ cup crumbled goat cheese

Freshly ground black pepper

This robust salad has all of the fall flavors that make us eagerly anticipate October each year. Butternut squash gets a quick roast until caramelized and tender, and is then tossed with crisp apple, creamy goat cheese, and hearty greens. Take a taste of the vinaigrette and you'll instantly be excited to eat this salad. If you're getting into the autumnal spirit, starting with this recipe is a no-brainer.

1 Preheat the oven to 450°F.

2 Add the squash to a large baking sheet with the olive oil, thyme, nutmeg, salt, and pepper. Toss to evenly coat and tuck the thyme sprigs under the squash cubes.

3 Roast for about 20 minutes, until slightly charred and tender. Set aside to cool to room temperature. Remove the thyme sprigs. Meanwhile, prep the salad and make the dressing.

4 **TO PREP THE SALAD:** To a large serving bowl, add the kale, brussels sprouts, and salt. Massage the vegetables for 15 to 20 seconds to encourage the salt to get into the fibers of the kale. Set aside.

5 **TO MAKE THE FIG VINAIGRETTE:** In a 16-ounce glass jar, combine the garlic, lemon juice, apple cider vinegar, mustard, fig jam, salt, pepper, and olive oil. Shake well to combine.

6 Top the kale and brussels sprouts with the red onion, apple, pumpkin seeds, goat cheese, and roasted butternut squash. Top with a few cracks of pepper, then drizzle the dressing on top. Toss to coat, and serve.

7 The salad will keep, dressed, for up to 5 days in the fridge.

TUSCAN KALE SALAD WITH LEMON TAHINI DRESSING

MAKES 8 SERVINGS

2 heads Tuscan kale, rinsed, stemmed, and chopped

½ teaspoon kosher salt

LEMON TAHINI VINAIGRETTE

⅓ cup tahini

2 garlic cloves, minced

1 tablespoon Dijon mustard

½ cup lemon juice (about 3 lemons)

2 teaspoons honey

¼ cup extra-virgin olive oil

¼ teaspoon kosher salt

1 fennel bulb, thinly sliced

2 red bell peppers, diced

1 (15-ounce) can chickpeas, drained and rinsed

4 green onions, white and green parts, thinly sliced

1 English cucumber, diced

¾ cup chopped toasted walnuts

This salad was the first of the Hungry Lady Salads I ever posted. The OG, the Queen, the one who started it all. Many of you have told me you could drink the lemon tahini vinaigrette, which is pretty much what I look for in a great salad dressing. The balance of nutty, creamy tahini, fresh lemon juice, sharp Dijon mustard, and honey is quite miraculous. Since originally posting the dressing, I've lowered the oil amount, as I've found it to be just as creamy and luscious without the full ½ cup. Feel free to switch up the salad ingredients themselves based on what you have on hand. Though I feel this hearty, crunchy combination makes the perfect salad, it really is all about the dressing with this one, and it would be very good to any salad you drizzle it on.

If your tahini is very smooth and "drippy," the dressing will come together easily in a mixing bowl. If it's thicker, a high-speed blender makes quick work of it.

1 Add the kale to a large bowl and massage the salt into the leaves to tenderize it. Leave the kale to sit while you make the dressing, or up to 4 hours.

2 **TO MAKE THE LEMON TAHINI VINAIGRETTE:** In a small bowl or blender, combine the tahini, garlic, mustard, lemon juice, honey, olive oil, and salt and whisk or blend until very smooth.

3 To the bowl of kale, add the fennel, bell peppers, chickpeas, green onions, cucumber, and walnuts.

4 Pour the vinaigrette over the salad and mix well. Serve, or refrigerate for up to 5 days.

ZUCCHINI PASTA SALAD WITH SUNDRIED TOMATOES AND MOZZARELLA

MAKES 6 SERVINGS

Kosher salt

3 medium zucchini

2 tablespoons extra-virgin olive oil, plus ⅓ cup

Freshly cracked black pepper

12 ounces gluten-free brown rice pasta (such as fusilli or penne)

1½ cups chopped mixed leafy herbs (such as basil, dill, parsley, and mint)

Zest and juice of ½ lemon

½ cup drained and chopped oil-packed sundried tomatoes

1 tablespoon capers, minced

2 bunches green onions, sliced thin

1 (8-ounce) ball fresh mozzarella, torn into chunks

I love this pasta salad, and I don't usually like pasta salad. Probably because this is more of a pasta dish in salad form, ya know? Zucchini, sundried tomatoes, mozzarella . . . all of these make great sense with pasta. A whole lot more sense than mayonnaise, in my humble opinion. Whether you love pasta salad or are a skeptic like me, this is a recipe you'll need when you're heading to a barbecue and thinking, *What can I bring?*

1 Bring a large pot of salted water to a boil. Preheat the oven to 450°F.

2 Slice the zucchini in half lengthwise and then crosswise into half-inch half-moons. On two large baking sheets, toss the zucchini slices with the 2 tablespoons of olive oil, 1 teaspoon of salt, and a few cracks of pepper. Roast for 12 to 14 minutes, rotating the pans halfway through. You want the zucchini browned but not mushy.

3 While the zucchini is cooling, cook the pasta according to package directions until al dente, then drain, rinse with cold water until cool, and add to a large serving bowl.

4 Add the herbs, lemon zest and juice, ½ teaspoon of salt, a few cracks of pepper, the ⅓ cup of olive oil, zucchini and any juices, sundried tomatoes, capers, green onions, and mozzarella. Stir gently together, taste, and add salt and pepper as needed. Serve. This is best eaten the same day.

WEEKNIGHTS

FIFTEEN-MINUTE TURMERIC-SPICED CHICKPEAS WITH SPINACH AND TOMATOES

MAKES 2 SERVINGS

1 tablespoon extra-virgin olive oil

1 medium onion, diced

2 garlic cloves, minced

¼ teaspoon ground cumin

1 teaspoon ground turmeric

½ teaspoon curry powder

Cayenne

1 tablespoon tomato paste

Kosher salt

⅛ teaspoon freshly cracked black pepper

1 (15-ounce) can chickpeas, drained and rinsed

1 medium tomato, diced

¼ cup full-fat coconut milk

1 (5-ounce) bag baby spinach

1 cup cooked long grain or brown rice (or cauliflower rice) for serving

2 tablespoons chopped fresh cilantro for serving

Can you tell by now that I love chickpeas? When I have a can of chickpeas in the pantry, I know I have dinner. They add heft and texture to salads, soups, and stews and take on bold ingredients so well.

This creamy, spicy vegan dish tastes like it's been cooking for hours, but it comes together in mere minutes. Don't be put off by the long ingredients list, because that's what supports the deep flavor development of this fifteen-minute dish.

I like to freeze extra coconut milk in ice cube trays so I always have some on hand for a filling, nutritious dinner like this one.

1 Heat the olive oil in a large, heavy saucepan over medium heat.

2 Add the onion and cook, stirring, for 3 to 4 minutes until softened. Add the garlic, cumin, turmeric, curry powder, ⅛ teaspoon of cayenne, the tomato paste, ½ teaspoon of salt, and the pepper. Cook, stirring, for 1 to 2 minutes until the mixture is fragrant and the tomato paste has darkened.

3 Add the chickpeas, ¼ cup water, and the tomato and bring to a simmer. Cover, lower the heat, and simmer for 5 minutes.

4 Stir in the coconut milk and all of the spinach. It will seem like too much spinach, but keep stirring and watch it wilt down quickly. Add another ¼ teaspoon of salt and simmer uncovered, stirring often, for 3 to 4 minutes until most of the liquid has evaporated. Taste, and add salt and/or cayenne if needed.

5 Serve over rice or cauliflower rice and top with cilantro.

A PERFECT STEAK WITH OLIVE PARSLEY VINAIGRETTE

MAKES 2 TO 4 SERVINGS

2 pounds New York strip steak or flat iron steak, cut into 2 large steaks

1 tablespoon neutral oil

Kosher salt

1 teaspoon freshly cracked black pepper

⅓ cup pitted green olives, sliced thin

1 garlic clove, grated

¼ teaspoon ground coriander

2 tablespoons red wine vinegar

3 tablespoons Worcestershire sauce

¼ cup chopped flat-leaf parsley

2 tablespoons extra-virgin olive oil

This is the best way to cook a steak. I will die on this hill. A sear in a hot pan finished by a trip to the oven results in an evenly cooked steak that has a beautiful crust and is tender inside (so long as you don't overcook it). To get the best crust, bring your steak to room temperature so it doesn't let off steam when it hits the pan the way a cold steak will, preventing the deep browning we are looking for. The olive parsley vinaigrette gives a brightness to the steak that I find rather refreshing. I think you will too.

1 Bring the steaks to room temperature before cooking, if possible. It will take about an hour.

2 Preheat the oven to 400°F.

3 Rub the steaks with the neutral oil, 2 teaspoons of salt, and the pepper, then let stand while you proceed.

4 In a small bowl, mix the olives, garlic, coriander, ¼ teaspoon of salt, the red wine vinegar, Worcestershire, parsley, and olive oil.

5 Heat a large cast-iron skillet over high heat.

6 If there is a fat cap on the edge of the steak, start by searing that for 2 to 3 minutes until browned. Then cook one side for 4 to 5 minutes until it is deeply caramelized.

7 Flip the steak over and immediately transfer the skillet to the oven for 6 to 10 minutes, depending on how you like your steak; 140 to 145°F will give you a medium-rare steak. Move the cooked steak to a cutting board and tent with foil, letting it rest for 10 minutes before slicing across the grain.

8 Pour any juices from the steak into the bowl with the olive vinaigrette and stir. Pour the vinaigrette onto the steaks as you serve.

AIR-FRYER OR OVEN-ROASTED HONEY MUSTARD SALMON

MAKES 4 SERVINGS

4 skin-on salmon fillets, about 6 ounces each

1 teaspoon kosher salt

⅛ teaspoon freshly cracked black pepper

1 tablespoon whole-grain mustard

1 tablespoon honey

2 garlic cloves, minced

½ teaspoon paprika

Juice of ½ lemon for serving

I use my air-fryer for only a handful of things. My motto is, use it only if it actually makes the recipe better, not just faster. Salmon is one of those things that is worth cooking in the air-fryer, and this Honey Mustard Salmon is one of those recipes that gets better in that appliance. The salty-sweet honey mustard glaze is a beautiful pair to salmon. The air-fryer does a sublime job of achieving a caramelized crust in less than 10 minutes without overcooking the fish. If you don't have an air-fryer, don't worry—there's an oven method included as well.

1 Season the salmon fillets with the salt and pepper on all sides.

2 In a small bowl, whisk together the mustard, honey, garlic, and paprika to make a glaze. Brush onto the sides and top of the salmon and air-fry at 400°F for 6 to 8 minutes, or until done to your liking. Top with a squeeze of lemon juice and serve.

OVEN INSTRUCTIONS

1 Preheat the oven to 450°F.

2 On a baking sheet lined with parchment paper, season the salmon fillets with the salt and pepper on all sides.

3 In a small bowl, whisk together the mustard, honey, garlic, paprika, and lemon juice.

4 Brush the glaze on the sides and top of the salmon and roast for 10 to 14 minutes, depending on the thickness of the fish and how well-done you like it. Serve.

ALMOST FAMOUS
CRISPY CRACKLE CHICKEN

MAKES 4 TO 6 SERVINGS

2	pounds boneless, skinless chicken breasts
	Kosher salt
¼	teaspoon freshly cracked black pepper
2	large eggs
1½	cups Fresh Bread Crumbs (page 260), dried, or panko-style bread crumbs
1	teaspoon garlic powder
2	tablespoons chopped fresh parsley
	Neutral oil for frying

"This is a chicken cutlet."

That is the comment that shows up again and again on this recipe, which holds the distinction of my most viral recipe to date.

Well, yes, this is a chicken cutlet. Why the fuss, then? Because it's lighter and crispier than your average chicken cutlet. The fresh bread crumbs are to thank for this, as is the shift away from flour. We dredge the chicken in egg and fresh bread crumbs seasoned with garlic and parsley, then pan-fry, which allows the coating to stick to the chicken better.

1   Butterfly the chicken breasts by slicing them horizontally, opening them like a book, and cutting through where they are still joined to get two chicken breast halves. Pat dry. If you'd like thinner cutlets, you can pound them using the flat side of a meat mallet. A neat way to do it is to place one half at a time either in a large freezer bag or between two pieces of plastic. Arrange the chicken on a large tray and season well on both sides with 2 teaspoons of salt and the pepper.

2   In one wide, shallow bowl, beat the eggs with a fork or whisk until very loose. Fill a second wide, shallow bowl with the bread crumbs and stir in the garlic powder and parsley. Dip each piece of chicken into the egg, let the excess drip off, then dip into the crumbs, pressing them on with your hands. Repeat with the remaining pieces of chicken, returning the coated pieces to the tray.

3   Pour just under ¼ inch of oil into a large frying pan and prepare plates lined with double paper for draining the chicken. Heat over medium-high until a droplet of water flicked into the pan hisses dramatically, or until the temperature of the oil is 350°F. Place your first few breaded cutlets in the oil—don't crowd them or it will lower the temperature, leading to heavier and greasier chicken. Cook the chicken, turning once, until it's a deep golden brown on both sides, 4 to 5 minutes for the first side and 3 to 4 minutes for the second.

4   Remove the cutlets from the pan to drain on the paper towels. Season right away, while still sizzling hot, with salt. Repeat with the remaining cutlets. Serve with anything: honey mustard, buffalo sauce, ketchup, marinara—it's all good.

CHIMICHURRI MEATBALLS

MAKES 25 TO 30 GOLF-BALL-SIZE MEATBALLS

CHIMICHURRI SAUCE

- 1 small shallot, peeled and cut into wedges
- 1 medium bunch flat-leaf parsley, stemmed
- 1 tablespoon fresh oregano leaves
- 2 garlic cloves, peeled
- 1 teaspoon kosher salt
- ½ teaspoon freshly cracked black pepper
- 2 tablespoons extra-virgin olive oil
- 1 tablespoon red wine vinegar

MEATBALLS

- Extra-virgin olive oil for greasing
- 2 pounds ground beef
- 2 large eggs
- 1 cup Fresh Bread Crumbs (page 260), dried
- 1 teaspoon kosher salt

Meatballs are a favorite in our family, and these herby, garlicky meatballs are on heavy rotation due partially to my kids' love for them. We've taken the Argentinian herb sauce chimichurri and put it not only on the meatballs but inside of them as well, giving us tons of flavor per bite. If you don't have a small food processor, feel free instead to chop everything finely and combine in a bowl. I like to make these with 85 percent lean ground beef rolled into little golf balls, perfect for spooning onto rice, alongside roasted broccolini. Be ready for these meatballs to be grabbed by little hands straight off the baking sheet before they even make it to the table.

1. **TO MAKE THE CHIMICHURRI SAUCE:** To a small food processor, add the shallot, parsley, oregano, garlic, salt, pepper, olive oil, and red wine vinegar. Pulse 8 to 10 times until finely chopped and combined, then set aside.

2. **TO MAKE THE MEATBALLS:** Preheat the oven to 425°F. Rub a large baking sheet lightly with olive oil.

3. Use clean hands to gently mix together the ground beef, eggs, bread crumbs, salt, and half of the chimichurri sauce, just until combined. Overworking it will result in tough meatballs. Roll the meat mixture into 1½-inch balls (about 2 tablespoons each) and place on the baking sheet. Leave an inch or two between each meatball to ensure they brown all over.

4. Bake for 10 to 12 minutes. Turn the oven to broil and cook for 5 to 7 minutes more until the meatballs are browned and have reached an internal temperature of 165°F on an instant-read thermometer. Discard any fat that has spilled into the pan. Transfer the meatballs to a serving platter, drizzle with the remaining half of the chimichurri sauce, and serve.

CREAMY FETA CHEESE SHRIMP WITH TOMATOES (SHRIMP SAGANAKI)

MAKES 2 TO 3 SERVINGS

2 tablespoons extra-virgin olive oil

½ medium onion, sliced thin

1 large fennel bulb, halved and sliced thin and 2 tablespoons chopped fronds reserved for garnish

2 garlic cloves, minced

Kosher salt

¼ teaspoon dried oregano

2 cups cherry tomatoes

⅛ teaspoon red pepper flakes

1 pound jumbo shrimp, peeled and deveined

4 ounces Greek or Bulgarian feta cheese, crumbled

This is another dinner recipe that is quick enough to make on a busy weeknight and elegant enough for a dinner party. This take on the classic Greek Shrimp Saganaki is a recipe I've been making for years, and the flavors are just beautiful together. The feta cheese added at the end melts ever so slightly, giving you a creamy, garlicky sauce filled with brightness from the fennel and tomatoes.

1 Heat the olive oil in a large, nonstick pan set over medium heat.

2 Sauté the onion for about 5 minutes, stirring, until softened. Add the fennel slices and garlic with a large pinch of salt and cook for 5 minutes, stirring occasionally. Add the oregano and stir for 10 seconds.

3 Add the tomatoes and red pepper flakes and cook for another 5 minutes, until the tomatoes just start to burst.

4 Add in the shrimp and a small pinch of salt and cook, stirring, for 3 to 5 minutes until the shrimp are pink. Add three-quarters of the feta and stir it in for about 1 minute.

5 To serve, ladle into shallow bowls and top with the reserved feta and fennel fronds.

GREEK CHICKEN SOUVLAKI

MAKES 6 SERVINGS ✳ ABOUT 10 SKEWERS

1 tablespoon finely minced fresh mint leaves

1 tablespoon finely minced fresh oregano (or 1 teaspoon dried)

3 garlic cloves, minced

2 tablespoons extra-virgin olive oil

2 teaspoons kosher salt

¼ teaspoon freshly cracked black pepper

2½ pounds boneless, skinless chicken breasts

Flaky sea salt for serving

Lemon wedges for serving

What is it about meat on a stick that just makes it more fun? Well . . . maybe because it's meat on a *stick*. Anyone who has seen the movie *There's Something About Mary* will appreciate what I'm saying here. With a simple, Greek-inspired marinade filled with fresh herbs and garlic, small bites of chicken breast take on great flavor and have extra insurance that they won't dry out the second they hit the heat. This is *the* summer barbecue recipe to double or even triple and serve with a quick tzatziki (Five-Minute Tzatziki, page 52) to feed a whole bunch of people without a whole bunch of work. Marinate the chicken a few hours before cooking and the majority of the work is already done by the time guests arrive.

1 In a large bowl, whisk together the mint, oregano, garlic, olive oil, salt, and pepper.

2 Cut the chicken into 1- to 2-inch pieces. Transfer to the bowl with the marinade. Cover the bowl and marinate in the fridge for 2 to 3 hours.

3 In a rimmed tray, soak bamboo skewers in water for 10 minutes to prevent burning.

4 When ready to cook, preheat the grill or grill pan to its highest setting (525°F or 550°F) or preheat the broiler to high for at least 10 minutes. Thread the chicken pieces onto ten 10- or 12-inch skewers.

5 If grilling, grill skewers for 3 minutes a side or until charred to your liking and the chicken registers 165°F on a meat thermometer. If broiling, broil on a baking sheet with rack for 4 to 5 minutes per side. Transfer to a platter.

6 Sprinkle with flaky sea salt. Serve with lemon wedges, Five-Minute Tzatziki (page 52), rice or pita, and some Quick Pickled Red Onions (page 262) if you have some.

HOT CHILI OIL NOODLES
WITH KALE CHIPS

MAKES 4 SERVINGS

6   cups packed curly kale

Kosher salt

2   tablespoons extra-virgin olive oil

14   ounces dried rice noodles

3   garlic cloves, grated

2   tablespoons sambal oelek (or any garlic chili sauce)

2   tablespoons toasted sesame oil

¼   cup reduced-sodium soy sauce

1   teaspoon rice wine vinegar

3   tablespoons neutral oil

2   green onions, white and green parts, sliced thin, for serving

In this twenty-minute recipe, rice noodles are tossed with a sizzling chili oil that coats each strand with slippery, savory perfection and then are topped with crispy kale chips that wilt slightly under the weight of the pasta. There is an incredible Asian market about half an hour away from me that I like to visit every other month to stock up on my favorite Asian ingredients like sambal oelek chile paste, rice wine vinegar, noodles, and of course soy sauce, but you can find these ingredients at most grocery stores now. On a chilly, windy autumn day there isn't much better than sitting down with this bowl of noodles resting in my lap in the family room and watching episodes of *Parenthood* that I've seen a thousand times before.

1   Place racks in the upper and lower thirds of the oven and preheat to 400°F.

2   Remove the kale ribs and discard. Rinse and pat dry the kale leaves and tear into 2-inch pieces. In a large bowl toss the kale, ½ teaspoon of salt, and the olive oil to coat. Divide the mixture evenly between two rimmed baking sheets and roast, tossing with a spatula and rotating baking sheets halfway through, until the kale is crisp and browned, 10 to 14 minutes.

3   While the kale chips are cooking, cook the noodles in a large pot of heavily salted boiling water according to package directions. Drain with a colander and rinse immediately under cold running water. Shake off any residual water and set the noodles aside.

4   To make the sauce, whisk together the garlic, sambal oelek, sesame oil, soy sauce, and rice wine vinegar in a large bowl (one large enough to fit the noodles and kale).

5   Heat the neutral oil in a small pan until tiny bubbles appear, then immediately pour it over the sauce in the large bowl and whisk it in quickly.

6   Dump in the noodles and the kale and mix well. Serve in bowls, with green onions, and with Netflix.

SAUSAGE AND PEPERONATA

MAKES 4 SERVINGS

3 tablespoons extra-virgin olive oil

2 pounds sweet Italian sausage, cut into 2-inch pieces on a diagonal

1 large yellow onion, diced

3 garlic cloves, smashed and sliced thin

4 red and/or orange bell peppers, seeded and sliced thin

2 large tomatoes, diced

½ teaspoon kosher salt

Freshly cracked black pepper

2 teaspoons balsamic vinegar (the best quality you have)

¼ cup minced fresh basil

1 tablespoon minced fresh oregano

This dish is a spin on the Italian classic of sausage and peppers, using the Calabrian pepper preparation (say that ten times fast) peperonata. Peppers, onion, and tomatoes are stewed with garlic, balsamic vinegar, and herbs, melting into a subtle sweet-sour condiment that is as good here with the sausage as it is on grilled bread with fresh mozzarella.

1 Heat 1 tablespoon of the olive oil in a large skillet, cast-iron preferred, over medium-high heat.

2 Add the cut sausages to the skillet and brown on both sides, 2 to 3 minutes per side. Transfer the browned sausages to a plate and set aside. Turn the heat to medium.

3 Add the remaining 2 tablespoons of olive oil to the skillet, then add the onion and sauté for 4 to 5 minutes until translucent. Add the garlic and cook for another 1 to 2 minutes.

4 Add the bell peppers and tomatoes to the skillet, turn the heat to medium-low, and season with the salt and a few cracks of pepper. Cook, stirring frequently, until everything gets very soft, about 30 minutes. Make sure to scrape the bottom of the pan as you stir to keep it from burning.

5 Add in the balsamic, basil, and oregano, then nestle the cooked sausages into the peperonata. Keep cooking for 2 to 3 minutes to heat through. Taste, and add salt and pepper if needed. Serve warm or at room temperature.

MISO-TERIYAKI PORK TENDERLOIN

MAKES 4 TO 6 SERVINGS

2 tablespoons pure maple syrup, the darker the better

¼ cup low-sodium soy sauce

2 tablespoons apple cider vinegar

2 tablespoons red or white miso

1 (1-inch) piece fresh ginger, peeled and minced

2 pork tenderloins, about 1.5 pounds each

2 tablespoons extra-virgin olive oil

1½ teaspoons kosher salt

¼ teaspoon freshly cracked black pepper

3 to 4 green onions, white and green parts sliced thin, for serving

Most store-bought teriyaki sauces are filled with sugar, and not only is that problematic for the nutrition of your meal, but it's problematic for the taste. Sugar should not be the dominant flavor in a teriyaki sauce.

By adding ingredients like miso paste, maple syrup, soy sauce, and ginger, you end up with a balanced, flavor-packed sauce you use to baste the pork not once, not twice, but three times. Make this recipe as directed during the colder months, or on the grill when the weather warms up. It's always a hit.

1 Preheat the oven to 400°F.

2 In a small saucepan, combine the syrup, soy sauce, vinegar, miso, 2 tablespoons of water, and the ginger. Bring to a boil over medium heat and simmer, whisking constantly, for 3 to 5 minutes until it's thickened enough to coat the back of a spoon. Let cool.

3 Rub the pork tenderloins with the olive oil, salt, and pepper.

4 Heat a large pan, cast-iron preferred, over medium-high heat, and when hot, sear the pork for 2 to 3 minutes on each side to brown.

5 Pour half of the sauce into a small dish and brush it all over the seared pork in the pan. Wash your brush—you will be saucing the pork two more times and want to avoid cross-contamination.

6 Roast for 18 to 22 minutes until a meat thermometer registers 145° to 150°F, depending on how thick your tenderloins are, halfway through brushing on more sauce from the bowl with a clean brush.

7 When the tenderloin is out of the oven, use a clean brush to apply the rest of the sauce in the pan that has not been touched.

8 Tent with aluminum foil and let cool for 15 minutes. Slice, sprinkle with green onions, and serve.

BAGNA CAUDA FISH

MAKES 4 SERVINGS

1 tablespoon extra-virgin olive oil

6 anchovy fillets, minced

2 garlic cloves, minced

¼ cup crème fraîche (or sour cream)

Zest and juice of ½ lemon

Freshly cracked black pepper

4 (8-ounce) fish fillets (such as cod, red snapper, or halibut)

Kosher salt

¼ cup chopped fresh parsley for serving

A fabulous dinner recipe that is easy enough to make on a Wednesday night yet sophisticated enough to serve at a weekend dinner party is a great thing to have in your back pocket. Bagna Cauda is a classic dish from Piedmont, Italy, of warm olive oil with anchovies and garlic served as an appetizer with crudites. This classic Italian flavor blend paired with roasted cod, halibut, or any whitefish is a match made in heaven.

1 To make the sauce, place the olive oil in a small sauté pan over medium-low heat. Add the anchovies and garlic and simmer, stirring, for 1 to 2 minutes until the anchovies have melted. Transfer to a small bowl and whisk in the crème fraîche, the lemon zest and juice, and several cracks of pepper. Set aside to cool.

2 Preheat the oven to 425°F.

3 Line a baking sheet with parchment paper. Place the fish fillets skin-side down on the sheet and pat them dry. Sprinkle generously with salt and pepper.

4 Spoon the sauce evenly over the fish fillets, making sure the fish is completely covered. Bake for 10 to 15 minutes, depending on the thickness of the fish, until it's barely done. (The fish will be opaque in color and the center will feel warm when it's done—insert a paring knife and touch it to your fingertip to make sure.) Serve hot or at room temperature with the sauce from the baking sheet spooned over the top. Finish with the parsley and serve.

ONE-POT PASTA WITH CHICKEN SAUSAGE AND BROCCOLI

MAKES 6 SERVINGS

Kosher salt

1 (8-ounce) head broccoli, cut into small florets

12 ounces brown rice pasta (such as farfalle or penne)

2 tablespoons extra-virgin olive oil

1 pound fresh chicken sausage, removed from casing

5 to 6 garlic cloves, minced

¼ cup freshly grated Parmesan cheese

¼ teaspoon red pepper flakes (optional)

Freshly cracked black pepper

As a busy mom, I'm a big fan of a pasta that is a full meal in a bowl, with veggies and meat included. The classic pasta dish of orecchiette, sausage, and broccoli rabe gets a lighter makeover here, with no flavor or satisfaction lost. Take a big bowl, grab yourself a big serving, and take big bites knowing you've got it all covered here.

1 Bring a large pot of heavily salted water to boil. While it's heating up, fill a large bowl with cold water and ice to make an ice bath.

2 Add the broccoli to the boiling water and blanch for about 30 seconds, then remove with a slotted spoon to the ice water.

3 Add the pasta to the same boiling water you cooked the broccoli in and cook according to package directions for al dente.

4 In a large high-sided sauté pan or Dutch oven, add 1 tablespoon of the olive oil and brown the sausage on medium-high heat, breaking up with a wooden spoon into small pieces as it cooks, 7 to 9 minutes. Set aside in a dish or a bowl.

5 Add the remaining 1 tablespoon of olive oil to the pan and cook the garlic, stirring, for about 30 seconds until just golden.

6 Return the broccoli to the pan, mix well with the garlic, and cook for a minute. Return the cooked sausage to the pan and mix well.

7 Drain the pasta, reserving 1 cup of pasta water, and add the pasta to the broccoli mixture. Lower the heat and stir for about 30 seconds. Add ½ cup of the pasta water, the Parmesan, and the red pepper flakes if using.

8 Adjust the salt and pepper to taste and toss for another 30 seconds so that everything is mixed well and the pasta is coated with the sauce. Add the rest of the pasta water if needed to create more sauce. Serve.

KALE AND FETA TURKEY BURGERS

MAKES 6 SERVINGS ✳ 12 BURGERS

8	ounces Tuscan kale
4	tablespoons extra-virgin olive oil
1	small yellow onion, grated
5	garlic cloves, minced
2	pounds ground dark turkey meat
⅔	cup crumbled feta cheese
2	teaspoons dried oregano
1	teaspoon kosher salt
½	teaspoon freshly cracked black pepper

I had yet to eat a turkey burger that didn't taste dry—until I made these. Not only are they not dry thanks to the dark turkey meat and fat from both the oil and the feta, but they are crave-worthy, with puddles of feta, garlic, and greens throughout. And don't worry about biting into a piece of raw kale—we cook it down with garlic and olive oil so it practically melts right in. These burgers are an easy and tasty dinner all year round, served on burger buns or over rice, or simply paired with salad or veggies.

1   Place a large skillet, cast-iron preferred, over medium heat.

2   Remove and discard the kale stems and finely chop the leaves. Add 2 tablespoons of the olive oil to the pan and once hot, add the onion and garlic. Cook, stirring, for 2 to 3 minutes until lightly browned. Add the kale and cook until it is wilted. Remove from the heat and let cool slightly before making the burgers.

3   In a large bowl, combine the ground turkey, feta, oregano, salt, and pepper. Mix gently with your hands or a rubber spatula just until combined.

4   Add the kale mixture to the turkey mixture and gently toss to distribute throughout. Spray your hands with a little cooking spray and form the mixture into ⅓-cup patties.

5   Heat the pan back up to medium heat.

6   Add the remaining 2 tablespoons of olive oil and, working in batches so as not to overcrowd the pan, pan-fry the patties for 3 to 4 minutes per side until well browned and cooked through (a meat thermometer should register a 160°F internal temperature).

7   Serve on buns, bunless with rice and vegetables, or with a simply dressed arugula salad.

ONE-PAN
JAMMY LEMON CHICKEN

MAKES 4 TO 6 SERVINGS

2 lemons

2 shallots, peeled and cut into thin wedges

Kosher salt

1 (8-ounce) bunch curly kale

2½ pounds bone-in, skin-on chicken thighs and/or breasts (4 to 6)

Freshly cracked black pepper

2 teaspoons chopped fresh rosemary

2 tablespoons extra-virgin olive oil

1 (15-ounce) can chickpeas, drained and rinsed

½ cup low-sodium chicken stock

A one-pan meal means less work, less mess, and less to juggle. In other words, an ideal weeknight dinner recipe. You can use all chicken breasts, all thighs, or a combination of breasts and thighs like I do here. A little tip: When using a combination, place the side of the pan with the thighs toward the back of the oven, where the temperature is hottest.

1 Preheat the oven to 450°F.

2 Slice one lemon in half crosswise, then into very thin half-moons and remove the seeds. Toss the shallots and lemon slices together in a small bowl with a pinch of salt. Remove the kale ribs and discard, then tear the leaves into large pieces. Set aside.

3 Pat the chicken dry with paper towels, making sure to get the skin as dry as possible. In a small bowl, mix together 2 teaspoons of salt, ½ teaspoon of pepper, and the rosemary. Loosen the chicken skin with your fingers and rub the rosemary mixture under the skin and on the bottoms of the chicken pieces. This will flavor the meat and also protect the rosemary from burning in the oven. Rub the chicken pieces with 1 tablespoon of the olive oil and let it sit while you continue.

4 Add the remaining 1 tablespoon of olive oil to a large ovenproof skillet set over medium heat.

5 Transfer the shallot and lemon, chickpeas, kale, ½ teaspoon of salt, and ⅛ teaspoon of pepper to the pan. Cut the remaining lemon in half and squeeze in the juice from one half. Cook, stirring, for 2 to 4 minutes.

6 Place the chicken pieces on top of the kale mixture and roast for 20 minutes. Pour the stock into the pan, around but not on the chicken, and roast for another 10 to 15 minutes until a meat thermometer inserted into the thickest part of the meat registers 155° to 160°F.

7 Remove the chicken from the oven, sprinkle it with the juice from the remaining lemon half, cover the skillet tightly with aluminum foil, and allow to rest for 5 to 10 minutes.

8 Serve the chicken, kale, and chickpeas with the jammy lemon slices on top.

ROASTED CAULIFLOWER TACOS *WITH* AVOCADO LIME CREMA

MAKES 4 SERVINGS

ROASTED CAULIFLOWER

1   (2½- to 3-pound) head cauliflower, broken into about 8 cups of florets

½   teaspoon sweet paprika

1   teaspoon chili powder

1   teaspoon onion powder

1   teaspoon kosher salt

2   tablespoons extra-virgin olive oil

AVOCADO LIME CREMA

1   large avocado, halved and pitted

½   cup chopped fresh cilantro

    Juice of 1 lime

¼   teaspoon kosher salt

8   corn tortillas, warmed

½   cup Quick Pickled Red Onions (page 262)

½   cup crumbled queso fresco

¼   cup chopped fresh cilantro

    Juice of 2 limes

If you've never tried roasting spiced cauliflower and putting it into a tortilla with a cool, creamy sauce, this is your nudge. This roasted cauliflower is a fantastic recipe in and of itself, but give it some avocado-lime crema action and it's on a whole other level. We aren't trying to pretend cauliflower is ground beef or carnitas here—we are honoring her for the versatile, hearty vegetable she is and having a grand old time doing it.

1   **TO MAKE THE ROASTED CAULIFLOWER:** Preheat the oven to 425°F.

2   Arrange the cauliflower florets on a large baking sheet and add the paprika, chili powder, onion powder, salt, and olive oil. Toss to coat evenly.

3   Roast for 35 to 45 minutes, stirring halfway through, until the cauliflower is browned all over.

4   **TO MAKE THE AVOCADO LIME CREMA:** While the cauliflower is roasting, scoop out the avocado flesh and add it to a blender with the cilantro, lime juice, and salt. Blend for a few seconds until smooth and creamy.

5   When the cauliflower is done, warm the tortillas by charring them on a gas grill open flame (holding each with tongs) or microwaving them for 20 seconds or so.

6   On each tortilla, spread the avocado lime crema, add the cauliflower, and top with pickled onions, queso fresco, cilantro, and lime juice. Serve right away.

SPICY FUSILLI WITH TOMATO AND CREAM

MAKES 4 SERVINGS

Kosher salt

1 tablespoon extra-virgin olive oil

1 medium yellow onion, diced

4 garlic cloves, peeled and smashed

1 (6-ounce) can tomato paste

½ teaspoon red pepper flakes

⅔ cup full-fat coconut milk (or heavy cream)

1 pound brown rice fusilli (or regular)

¾ cup freshly grated Parmesan cheese

Fresh basil for serving (optional)

I first cooked this dish for a high-profile family back in 2011 to rave reviews. It wasn't until after they enjoyed the meal that they found out that the "creaminess" of the sauce was actually coconut milk. With all of the deep, savory flavors of tomato paste and garlic, there wasn't a hint of coconut to be detected. If you'd like, use heavy cream, which of course will work beautifully.

1 Bring a large pot of heavily salted water to a boil.

2 Adjacent to your stockpot, heat the olive oil in a large, deep skillet over medium heat. Add the onion and garlic and cook, stirring, for about 5 minutes.

3 Add the tomato paste and red pepper flakes and stir. Continue to cook, with consistent stirring, until the tomato paste starts to brown on the bottom of the pot. This will take about 5 minutes. Add a splash of water to deglaze the pan and scrape up the browned bits.

4 Add in the coconut milk or heavy cream and 1 teaspoon of salt. Stir constantly until a smooth sauce forms.

5 Turn off the heat and cover with a lid.

6 Add the fusilli to the pot of boiling salted water and cook for 2 minutes less than the package directions require. You want it to be a bit less than al dente. Scoop out 1 cup of the pasta water and set aside.

7 Uncover the skillet of sauce and turn the heat on low. Using a slotted spoon, add the fusilli to the sauce.

8 Add ½ cup of the pasta water to the sauce and stir to combine, then add ½ cup of the Parmesan, stirring to melt the cheese.

9 Stream in as much of the leftover ½ cup of pasta water as needed to give you the right consistency.

10 Serve the pasta topped with the remaining ¼ cup Parmesan and basil, if desired.

SOUPS

+

STEWS

"GET WELL" CHICKEN AND RICE SOUP

MAKES 8 SERVINGS

3 tablespoons extra-virgin olive oil

1 medium onion, chopped

3 celery stalks, cut into ½-inch pieces

3 carrots, cut into ½-inch pieces

3 garlic cloves, minced

1 teaspoon thyme leaves (from 4 sprigs)

Kosher salt

Freshly cracked black pepper

2 tablespoons gluten-free all-purpose flour

1 cup (5 ounces) white rice

8 cups chicken stock (homemade or low-sodium)

4 cups bite-size pieces of roasted chicken or turkey

Juice of ½ lemon

¼ cup chopped fresh parsley for serving

Have a family member who is sick? Make this soup. Have a friend who just had a baby? Make this soup. Have a chill in your bones from a blustery winter day? Make this soup.

It's an excellent way to repurpose leftover chicken, or even turkey from Thanksgiving when you just can't look at another plate of stuffing and cranberry sauce.

1 In a large stockpot, warm the olive oil over medium heat. Add the onion and cook, stirring, for 5 minutes. Add the celery, carrots, garlic, thyme, 1 teaspoon of salt, and ¼ teaspoon of pepper. Cook, stirring occasionally, until the vegetables start to soften, about 5 minutes. Sprinkle the flour over the vegetables and cook, stirring, until evenly coated and lightly browned, about 3 minutes.

2 Add the rice to the stockpot, and gradually stir in the stock and 2 cups of water. Bring to a boil, then turn the heat to low, stirring occasionally, until the vegetables are tender, about 10 minutes. Add the chicken and simmer, stirring occasionally, until the rice is tender, 5 to 10 minutes longer. Turn off the heat and stir in the lemon juice.

3 Taste for salt and pepper and add more if needed. Ladle the soup into bowls, top with parsley, and serve.

NOTE *If you're planning to eat this over the course of a few days, cook the rice separately and add it to the soup when you reheat it. Starches have a tendency to drink up the liquid as they sit.*

CHARRED CAULIFLOWER AND POTATO SOUP WITH LEMON

MAKES 4 SERVINGS

1 (1½- to 2-pound) head cauliflower, separated into small florets

6 garlic cloves, unpeeled

4 tablespoons extra-virgin olive oil

Kosher salt

Freshly cracked black pepper

1 large yellow onion, diced

¼ teaspoon red pepper flakes

1 medium (about 8-ounce) russet potato, peeled and thinly sliced

4 cups vegetable stock (homemade or low-sodium)

Juice and zest of 1 lemon

⅓ cup freshly grated Parmesan cheese

¼ cup chopped fresh parsley

I just love when a recipe so humble surprises me with so much depth of flavor. Roasting the cauliflower and garlic gives the soup a deep caramelization and flavor, and the potato melts into the broth and provides texture to the dish. Finished with Parmesan and lemon, it's a homey soup that still surprises me with its greatness.

1 Preheat the oven to 450°F.

2 On two large baking sheets, toss the cauliflower and garlic cloves with 2 tablespoons of the olive oil, 1 teaspoon of salt, and ¼ teaspoon of black pepper. Roast for 15 to 20 minutes until browned and tender. Remove the skin from the garlic and discard it, then return the garlic to the cauliflower. Set aside.

3 Add the remaining 2 tablespoons of olive oil to a large pot set over medium heat.

4 Add the onion, red pepper flakes, and ½ teaspoon of salt. Cook for 3 to 4 minutes to soften the onion. Add the potato to the pot with the vegetable stock and 1 teaspoon of salt. Bring the soup to a simmer, cover the pot, and cook until the potato is just tender, about 15 minutes. Add the cauliflower and garlic, cover again, and cook for another 5 minutes to marry the flavors. Taste the broth and add salt if needed.

5 If using an immersion blender, blend the soup until it's smooth in some places but still quite chunky in others. If using a high-speed blender, transfer half the soup, blend until smooth, and add back to the other half. Continue blending if you want it very smooth. Stir in the lemon juice and zest. Finish with Parmesan, pepper, and parsley, and serve.

CREAMY ROASTED TOMATO SOUP WITH RYE CROUTONS

MAKES 4 SERVINGS

4   (1-inch-thick) slices of rye bread, cubed

Extra-virgin olive oil

Kosher salt

8   medium tomatoes, halved and seeded

1   yellow onion, quartered

4   garlic cloves, smashed gently and skins intact

1   (4-inch) piece fresh ginger, in its skin

½   teaspoon ground coriander

Freshly cracked black pepper

⅓   cup chopped fresh parsley

1   cup full-fat coconut milk, plus a bit of the cream for serving

1   teaspoon apple cider vinegar

1   cup vegetable stock (homemade or low-sodium)

Tomato soup was never a favorite of mine. I never really understood the fuss—quite frankly, it felt like more of a condiment to a grilled cheese sandwich than a soup worth raving about. If you feel like I used to about tomato soup, this recipe will change your mind. By slow-roasting the tomatoes until they're sticky-sweet, you get such fantastic flavor. Ginger and coriander brighten up what can often feel like a one-note soup. A bit of coconut milk to provide some cream, and you have a vegan soup that's at once vibrant and comforting. I like rye bread for the croutons, but any hearty bread will do.

1   Preheat the oven to 300°F.

2   On a large baking sheet, toss the bread cubes with 1 tablespoon of olive oil and ½ teaspoon of salt until well coated.

3   Bake for 15 to 20 minutes until the bread is dried and golden. Reserve for serving.

4   On a baking sheet, place the tomatoes cut-sides up, along with the onion, garlic cloves, and ginger. Sprinkle the coriander, ¼ teaspoon of pepper, and 1½ teaspoons of salt over the onion and tomato, and drizzle the whole tray with ¼ cup of olive oil. Roast in the oven for 90 minutes, stirring halfway through.

5   Take the baking sheet out of the oven, peel the skin off the ginger, and squeeze the garlic out of the skins. Discard the skins.

6   Add the roasted vegetables to a high-speed blender, followed by the coconut milk, apple cider vinegar, and vegetable stock. Blend until the soup is smooth and a bright orange color, scraping down the sides as needed with a rubber spatula. Taste, and add salt and pepper if needed. Transfer the soup to a large pot over medium-high heat and bring to a gentle simmer.

7   Ladle into bowls. Top with a few drops of coconut cream and the rye croutons and serve. Leftovers can be refrigerated for up to 5 days.

ROASTED PUMPKIN SOUP
WITH APPLE, CURRY,
AND HAZELNUTS

MAKES 4 TO 6 SERVINGS

1   (2½- to 3-pound) sugar pumpkin
     (or 1 butternut squash)

3   tablespoons extra-virgin olive oil

     Kosher salt

     Freshly cracked black pepper

1   small sweet, tart apple (Honeycrisp
     or Pink Lady)

1   medium yellow onion

3   garlic cloves, unpeeled

1½   teaspoons curry powder

1   (13.5-ounce) can full-fat coconut
     milk, some reserved for drizzling

½   cup vegetable stock (homemade or
     low-sodium)

½   teaspoon apple cider vinegar

½   cup chopped roasted hazelnuts for
     serving

Don't be scared off by the thought of roasting a pumpkin. If you can roast butternut squash, you can roast a pumpkin. In fact, it's a great way to put those post-Halloween pumpkins to use. The trick I share for easily cutting into pumpkin and squash deems this recipe worth making alone, but the sublime combination of squash, apple, curry, and hazelnuts makes this *the* go-to end-of-October soup.

1   Make room in the oven by moving both racks to the lowest positions and then preheat to 400°F.

2   To make the pumpkin easy to cut, place it whole in the oven for 10 to 15 minutes to soften slightly. Cut it in half and scoop out the insides, discarding the strings and seeds or saving them to roast later. Place the pumpkin cut-sides up on a large baking sheet.

3   Drizzle the pumpkin with 2 tablespoons of the olive oil and sprinkle with 1 teaspoon of salt and ¼ teaspoon of pepper.

4   Roast for 20 minutes, then flip and roast with cut-sides down for 20 to 30 minutes more, or until the flesh is soft. Remove from the oven, let cool, then peel the skin away from the flesh.

5   While the pumpkin roasts, slice the apple and onion into wedges and arrange on a baking sheet with the garlic cloves in their skin. Top with the curry powder. Drizzle with the remaining 1 tablespoon of olive oil and ¼ teaspoon of salt.

6   Roast for 20 minutes, or until the edges turn golden brown and everything is tender. Remove the skins from the garlic and discard.

7   Working in batches, add the pumpkin flesh, roasted onion, apple, garlic, coconut milk, ¼ cup of the stock, the apple cider vinegar, and 1 teaspoon of salt to a high-speed blender. Puree until silky smooth, scraping the sides of the blender as needed, then transfer to a large bowl. If it's too thick, add the rest of the stock to thin and blend again. Taste, and add more salt if needed.

8   Serve in shallow soup bowls with chopped hazelnuts, a few
cracks of pepper, and a drizzle of coconut milk.

9   Store leftovers in the fridge for up to 5 days.

VEGAN RED LENTIL SOUP WITH GINGER AND LIME

MAKES 4 SERVINGS

1 lime (preferably organic)

2 tablespoons extra-virgin olive oil

4 garlic cloves, minced

1 tablespoon peeled and minced fresh ginger

1 large yellow onion, diced

2 celery stalks, diced

1 teaspoon ground cumin

1 teaspoon ground coriander

⅛ teaspoon cayenne

4 cups vegetable stock (homemade or low-sodium)

1 (15-ounce) can diced tomatoes

1 cup dried red lentils, rinsed

  Kosher salt

2 green onions, white and green parts, sliced thin, for serving

¼ cup chopped fresh cilantro for serving

This soup is proof that hot soup can also be bright and energizing. It comes together in 30 minutes, making it easy enough for a weeknight dinner—you only need to add some crusty bread to make a full meal for the table. The whole lime slices become soft and tender, and are meant to be eaten rind and all. You of course can remove them if that's too much of a stretch. I love the way both the lemon and fresh ginger offer an upswing to the deep, earthy spices, and the cilantro and green onion topping brings so much freshness to the soup. It's really a happy bowl of goodness.

1 Cut the lime in half, reserving one half for finishing the soup. Slice the half you are using now into very thin rounds. Set aside.

2 In a medium pot, heat the olive oil over medium heat.

3 Add the garlic, ginger, onion, and celery and sauté for 3 to 5 minutes until they soften. Add the cumin, coriander, and cayenne and cook for 30 seconds more.

4 Add the stock, 2 cups of water, the tomatoes, sliced lime, lentils, and ½ teaspoon of salt. Cover the pot and bring to a boil.

5 Lower the heat and simmer the soup for 25 to 30 minutes until the lentils are cooked and the flavors have deepened.

6 Taste, and add salt if needed. If you're using unsalted stock, it will be needed.

7 If you'd prefer not to eat the lime slices with their rind, remove them now. Serve the soup ladled into shallow bowls, sprinkled with the green onions and cilantro, and finished with a squeeze of lime.

WATERMELON GAZPACHO

MAKES 4 TO 6 SERVINGS ✳ 2 QUARTS

1　(1-inch) piece fresh ginger, peeled

7　cups diced watermelon (a 5- to 6-pound watermelon)

½　English cucumber, halved, seeded, and diced small

1　yellow bell pepper, diced

2　large ripe tomatoes, seeded and diced

3　celery stalks, diced

4　green onions, white and green parts sliced thin

　Juice of 2 limes

2　to 4 tablespoons apple cider vinegar

¼　cup extra-virgin olive oil

1　teaspoon kosher salt

3　to 4 sprigs mint leaves, chopped

This is not your average gazpacho. Yes, it has all of the bright crunch and refreshing taste of the classic cold Spanish-style soup, but with watermelon added, it somehow also becomes something entirely different. It's still a savory soup, but with an intoxicating sweet note that makes it almost addictive. Serve this for lunch when the heat is relentless and the thought of turning on the oven is too much to bear, or in little cocktail glasses at a dinner party. Your guests will rave, I assure you.

1　Place the ginger and 4 cups of the watermelon in a high-powered blender and puree. This will yield 3 to 4 cups of puree.

2　Transfer the puree to a large bowl. Add the remaining 3 cups of diced watermelon and the cucumber, bell pepper, tomatoes, celery, green onions, lime juice, 2 tablespoons of the apple cider vinegar, the olive oil, salt, and mint. Stir to combine. Taste. Adjust with more lime, apple cider vinegar, and/or salt to taste. Cover the gazpacho and refrigerate until very cold, at least 1 hour and up to 4 hours.

3　When ready to serve, divide the gazpacho among small glasses or bowls. Serve.

WHITE BEAN AND CHICKEN SAUSAGE SOUP WITH GREENS

MAKES 6 TO 8 SERVINGS

1 tablespoon extra-virgin olive oil

1 large onion, diced

3 garlic cloves, minced

2 large carrots, peeled and diced

12 ounces chicken sausage, sliced and cut into half-moons

Kosher salt

1 teaspoon ground cumin

1 teaspoon sweet paprika

½ teaspoon ground ginger

¼ teaspoon red pepper flakes

1 tablespoon tomato paste

1 (28-ounce) can whole tomatoes, crushed

2 (15-ounce) cans white beans, drained and rinsed

6 cups vegetable stock (homemade or low-sodium)

4 cups packed raw spinach

Juice of ½ lemon

Freshly cracked black pepper

Fresh parsley leaves for garnish

I posted this hearty, savory soup recipe in January 2022 and called it the Hungry Lady Soup, because it's a full meal in a bowl and so very satisfying. The response to this soup was tremendous, and it went over just as well with the hungry ladies as it did with the hungry husbands and hungry children it was served to. I thought to myself, "My salads are the same sort of thing—they are Hungry Lady Salads!" I suppose I have this soup to thank for the salad fandom that would soon enter my world. So please, Hungry Lady Soup, accept this sincere expression of gratitude and forgive me for waiting so long to give it.

For the chicken sausage, I particularly like the Seemore and Bilinski's brands, and have used plain, Italian style, and the feta and spinach variety, all to great results.

1 In a large stockpot, heat the olive oil over medium heat.

2 Add the onion, garlic, and carrots, and sauté for 5 minutes until soft.

3 Add the chicken sausage and continue to cook until browned, 3 to 5 minutes.

4 Add 1 teaspoon of salt and the cumin, paprika, ginger, red pepper flakes, and tomato paste, and stir for another minute until fragrant.

5 Add the tomatoes and white beans, then add the stock, and water if needed, to cover.

6 Put the lid on the pot and bring the soup to a boil. Lower the heat and simmer for 20 to 25 minutes, covered.

7 Taste, and add salt if needed. It will be needed if you have used homemade, unsalted stock. Stir in the spinach and lemon juice and turn off the heat. The spinach will wilt quite quickly.

8 To serve, ladle into shallow bowls and top with black pepper and fresh parsley.

9 The soup will keep covered in the refrigerator for up to 5 days and in the freezer for up to 3 months.

WILD MUSHROOM AND BARLEY SOUP

MAKES 4 TO 6 SERVINGS

1 cup dried wild mushrooms

1 tablespoon extra-virgin olive oil

1 small onion, finely chopped

2 carrots, peeled and thinly sliced

2 celery stalks, thinly sliced

1 pound (about 2 cups) cremini or white button mushrooms, thinly sliced

1 tablespoon tomato paste

Kosher salt

Freshly cracked black pepper

4 cups beef stock (homemade or low-sodium)

6 sprigs thyme

1 heaping cup barley

¼ cup fresh parsley leaves for garnish

Mushroom and barley soup is one of my favorite soups ever, and it has been since I was a child. Mushrooms are very meaty, and when combined with chewy barley make for a soul-satisfying base to this soup. The combination of dried and fresh mushrooms is truly necessary here: You just won't achieve the deep flavor we are after with fresh mushrooms alone. I often use instant barley for this soup, which cooks in just 10 minutes, making this a breeze to whip up for a winter dinner on a school night and serve with crusty bread.

1 In a small bowl, combine the dried mushrooms with 3 cups of boiling water. Set aside to soak for 15 minutes to reconstitute while you make the rest of the soup.

2 In a large Dutch oven or heavy-bottomed pot, heat the oil over medium heat. Add the onion, carrots, and celery and cook, stirring, for 5 minutes until the onion is softened.

3 Add the fresh mushrooms and tomato paste with 1 teaspoon of salt and 1 teaspoon of pepper and cook, stirring, for 1 to 2 minutes until the tomato paste has caramelized and turned deep red.

4 Remove the wild mushrooms from their soaking liquid and add to the pot, discarding any hard pieces and reserving the liquid.

5 Cover the vegetable mixture with the stock and mushroom soaking liquid, along with the thyme sprigs. Notice that we aren't seasoning much yet with salt and pepper, but we will. Bring to a boil, stir in the barley, and lower the heat to medium-low. Cover the pot partially to simmer for 30 minutes. If using instant barley, add it when there is the same amount of time left for the soup as it takes to cook. Halfway through the simmer, taste the broth and add salt and pepper as needed. When the soup is fully cooked, remove the thyme sprigs and ladle into bowls, garnish with parsley, and serve.

FRENCH ONION SOUP, THE EASY WAY

1   tablespoon unsalted butter

4   large yellow onions, peeled and thinly sliced (about 9 cups)

    Kosher salt

2   garlic cloves, minced

1   teaspoon gluten-free or all-purpose flour

⅔   cup dry white wine

5   cups chicken stock (homemade or low-sodium)

1   teaspoon Worcestershire sauce

4   sprigs thyme

    Freshly cracked black pepper

    Sourdough baguette or French bread, cut into 8 (½-inch) slices

2   tablespoons extra-virgin olive oil

1   cup grated Gruyère cheese

French onion soup seems to be the thing that people order at restaurants and don't make at home. Maybe it's because it never tastes quite as good at home (you probably haven't been cooking your onions for long enough), or maybe it's because the "soup bowls under the broiler" bit feels intimidating. I've got a workaround for that here, by toasting the bread and then broiling it with cheese separately. It's a breeze to put it together before serving. Don't worry if the cheese has hardened before you're ready to eat. When you ladle the hot soup over the top, it'll warm back up for you.

1   In a large heavy-bottomed pot or Dutch oven, melt the butter over medium-low heat. Add the onions and sauté until deeply caramelized, 35 to 40 minutes, initially stirring every 3 to 5 minutes and then about once a minute toward the end. If the onions get too dark, turn the heat down to low . . . we want to cook low and slow with consistent stirring to bring out that caramelized onion magic. Add ¼ teaspoon of salt for the last few minutes of cooking.

2   Meanwhile, preheat the oven to 350°F.

3   When the onions are caramelized, add the garlic and sauté for 2 minutes. Stir in the flour and cook for an additional 1 minute.

4   Turn the heat to medium-high and stir in the wine to deglaze the pan, using a wooden spoon to scrape up any browned bits on the bottom.

5   Add the stock, 1 to 2 teaspoons of salt depending on if your stock is salted or not, the Worcestershire, and thyme sprigs and stir to combine. Bring to a simmer, then lower the heat to medium-low, cover, and simmer for at least 10 minutes. Stir in ½ teaspoon of pepper.

continues

6 **WHEN IT'S ALMOST READY, PREPARE THE CHEESY GARLIC TOASTS:** Brush the slices of bread with the olive oil and sprinkle lightly with salt. Place on a large baking sheet and bake for 5 to 7 minutes until golden brown. Remove from the oven and turn the broiler to high. Generously sprinkle the cheese evenly over the bread slices and cook under the broiler for 2 to 3 minutes to melt the cheese and brown it in places.

7 To serve, discard the thyme sprigs. Taste the soup and season with salt and pepper as needed. Ladle the soup into bowls, filling them three-quarters full, and top with one or two of the cheese toasts. Ladle a bit of soup on top of the toasts and serve.

SCRAPPY SLOW-COOKER CHICKEN STOCK

MAKES 4 TO 6 QUARTS

3 pounds leftover chicken bones, cooked, raw, or a combination

2 to 3 cups onions (tops, bottoms, skins)

2 to 3 cups celery (tops, bottoms)

2 to 3 cups carrots (tops, bottoms, skins)

¼ cup garlic (tops, bottoms, skins)

1 small bunch herb stems (thyme and parsley in particular)

1 tablespoon apple cider vinegar

1 tablespoon whole black peppercorns

2 dried bay leaves

I quite literally am never without this stock in my freezer. Homemade chicken stock is the foundation to so many recipes from soups and stews to casseroles and steamed vegetables, and once I made it in the slow cooker I never went back to the stovetop. I usually dump the chicken bones, vegetable scraps, and aromatics into the slow cooker right after a roast chicken dinner and wake up to rich stock ready to be portioned out and frozen. I like to leave it unsalted so that I can control that piece in the recipe I'm using it with. My MO is to keep a gallon-size plastic bag in the freezer and gradually fill it with vegetable scraps and chicken bones from rotisserie chickens we've enjoyed. Once the bag is full, it's time to make stock. Cooking it for longer than you think you should provides a deeply flavored stock. I was once told that the chicken bones should look like they've been washed up onto the beach—this checks out for me. Freeze the stock in large ice cube trays and lidded containers so you have it portioned out and ready to go. Talk about making something from nothing . . .

1 In a large slow cooker, combine the chicken bones, onions, celery, carrots, garlic, and herb stems. Cover it all with water by an inch or two, then add the apple cider vinegar, peppercorns, and bay leaves. The vinegar helps to draw nutrients out of the chicken bones.

2 Set the slow cooker to low and let it cook for 20 to 24 hours for the richest stock.

3 When it's done, turn off the slow cooker and let the stock cool for 30 minutes to make it safe to handle. Ladle the stock, bones and all, into a fine-mesh colander set over a very large bowl.

4 The stock will run through into the bowl, making it easy to discard the scraps. Let it cool to room temperature before refrigerating for up to 5 days or packing into plastic containers or bags and freezing for up to 3 months.

5 Use in everything!

SNOW DAY BEEF AND VEGETABLE STEW WITH PASTA

MAKES 6 SERVINGS

¼	pound bacon, diced small
1	small onion, diced
4	carrots, peeled and diced medium
6	garlic cloves, minced
1½	pounds ground beef (85% lean)
	Kosher salt
1½	cups red wine
5	to 6 cups beef stock (homemade or low-sodium)
1	(14.5-ounce) can diced tomatoes
4	bay leaves
3	cups packed fresh spinach
2	cups shredded green cabbage
8	ounces gluten-free cavatappi or elbow macaroni (or regular)
⅓	cup freshly grated Parmesan cheese

Snow falls, stew goes on the stove. That's typically how it goes around my house. This delicious stew is incredibly simple to make considering how much great stuff is in here.

Any dish that has beef, bacon, and red wine in the ingredients list is almost guaranteed to have great flavor, and this is no exception. The tender, slippery pasta and plentiful shreds of cabbage bulk it up even further, keeping you cozy and warm on the coldest of days.

1 Place the bacon in a large cold Dutch oven.

2 Turn the heat to medium-low and slowly cook the bacon until crispy and the fat is rendered, 7 to 9 minutes.

3 To the bacon, add the onion, carrots, and garlic. Cook, stirring, in the bacon fat for 3 to 4 minutes until lightly softened.

4 Add the ground beef and a large pinch of salt and cook until browned, 5 to 7 minutes, breaking it up with a wooden spoon.

5 Add the red wine, 5 cups of the stock, the tomatoes, and the bay leaves and bring to a boil. Lower the heat and simmer, partially covered, for 20 minutes.

6 Add the spinach and cabbage to the pot along with another teaspoon of salt and cook for another 20 minutes, adding the pasta for the last eight minutes to cook until al dente. Add the extra cup of stock if you need more liquid.

7 Taste, and add more salt if needed.

8 Remove the bay leaves and serve in shallow bowls, topped with Parmesan.

SWEET POTATO AND BLACK BEAN CHILI

MAKES 6 SERVINGS

- 1 tablespoon extra-virgin olive oil
- 1 large yellow onion, diced
- 1 pound sweet potatoes, peeled and diced into ¾-inch cubes (4 cups)
- 3 garlic cloves, minced

  Kosher salt
- 1 to 2 jalapeños, seeded and minced (leave in the seeds for more heat)
- 1 tablespoon ground cumin
- 2 tablespoons chili powder
- 1 teaspoon smoked paprika
- ½ teaspoon dried oregano
- 1 (14.5-ounce) can diced tomatoes
- 2 (14.5-ounce) cans black beans, drained and rinsed
- 3 cups vegetable stock (homemade or low-sodium)
- 1 large avocado
- ¼ cup chopped fresh cilantro
- 1 lime

Chili purists will shake their head at any chili that is made without . . . gasp . . . MEAT! Let them.

I love a classic chili, don't get me wrong, but sometimes I want something lighter while still fitting the flavor profile bill. The slight sweetness of the potatoes is a beautiful contrast to the savory beans and spicy broth, and topped with cool hunks of avocado and lime, it's a perfectly balanced soup that will keep carnivores and herbivores alike coming back for more.

1   In a large stockpot or Dutch oven, heat the olive oil over medium heat.

2   Add the onion and cook, stirring, for 2 to 3 minutes, then add the sweet potatoes, garlic, and 1 teaspoon of salt.

3   Keep sautéing until the onions are translucent and the sweet potatoes start to soften, 8 to 10 minutes.

4   Add the jalapeños, cumin, chili powder, paprika, and oregano. Heat until the spices are very fragrant, about a minute. Add the tomatoes, beans, and stock.

5   When the broth is bubbling, lower the heat and simmer, uncovered, for approximately 30 minutes, or until the sweet potatoes are totally tender. Season to taste with salt.

6   If serving right away, slice the avocado and distribute on each bowl of chili, with a sprinkle of cilantro and a large squeeze of lime.

7   If you have the time, refrigerate the chili for a few hours before reheating and the flavors will deepen even more.

SUNDAY SUPPERS

CHEESY EGGPLANT AND LENTIL BAKE

MAKES 6 TO 8 SERVINGS

Kosher salt

2 medium-large eggplants
(1½ pounds total), sliced crosswise
into ½-inch disks

2 tablespoons extra-virgin olive oil

1 large yellow onion, diced

3 garlic cloves, minced

2 teaspoons ground coriander

2 teaspoons paprika

½ teaspoon red pepper flakes

1 teaspoon dried oregano

8 ounces green lentils, cooked
according to package directions

1 (28-ounce) can diced tomatoes

Freshly cracked black pepper

2 cups grated mozzarella

Fresh parsley for serving

The Modern Casserole. That's what this is, halfway between Eggplant Parmesan and a lentil stew, if you will. Or maybe a lentil lasagna? Anyway . . . it is cheesy, meaty, and satisfying while also being vegetarian.

You can use any lentils you have lying around, even pre-cooked lentils from the grocery store, which are becoming more and more available. The texture will be softer, but it won't be any less delicious.

1 Preheat the oven to 350°F.

2 Bring a large pot of generously salted water to a boil.

3 Add the eggplant disks and boil for 5 to 7 minutes until soft but not mushy. Drain and set aside, patting dry to remove as much water as possible.

4 In a large pot set over medium heat, heat the olive oil, then add the onion and sauté for 2 to 3 minutes until lightly browned.

5 Add the garlic, coriander, paprika, red pepper flakes, oregano, and 1 teaspoon salt and cook for 2 minutes more.

6 Add the cooked lentils and tomatoes, along with a large pinch each of salt and pepper and stir, cooking for another 5 to 7 minutes.

7 Spread some of the lentil mixture on the bottom of a 9 by 13-inch casserole dish. Add half of the eggplant circles, followed by a third of the cheese.

8 Repeat these layers and finish with the last third of cheese.

9 Bake for about 30 minutes until warmed through and bubbling.

10 Finish with fresh parsley and let it stand for 15 minutes before scooping out into shallow bowls for serving.

CRISPY COD CAKES WITH TARTAR SAUCE

MAKES 4 TO 6 SERVINGS ✳ 10 TO 12 CAKES

1   pound russet or Idaho potatoes (about 2 medium potatoes)

    Kosher salt

1   pound cod fillets

1   teaspoon Old Bay seasoning

¼   teaspoon freshly cracked black pepper

1   tablespoon extra-virgin olive oil

2   large eggs

½   medium red bell pepper, diced small

¼   cup finely grated sweet onion

2   tablespoons chopped fresh parsley

¼   cup gluten-free all-purpose flour

TARTAR SAUCE

⅓   cup mayonnaise

1   tablespoon lemon juice

2   tablespoons dill pickle relish

1   teaspoon whole-grain mustard

1   tablespoon rinsed and minced capers

⅛   teaspoon freshly cracked black pepper

    Neutral oil for frying

    Lemon wedges for serving

If you like crab cakes, you'll love these crispy cod-and-potato cakes. They are tender and hearty inside, with a golden crust on the outside and served alongside a quick homemade tartar sauce. Do not be put off by the multiple steps: once you start, you'll see these are seamless to make, especially if you have cooked fish and potato before. I often use leftover potatoes and/or fish for this recipe as a way to reinvent leftovers, but I've included the instructions to make it all from scratch. They are so very worth making either way.

1   Preheat the oven to 300°F.

2   Peel and dice the potatoes, place them into a pot of cold salted water, then bring to a boil.

3   Cook for 10 to 15 minutes until tender, then drain and mash them with a fork in the pan. Set aside to cool.

4   Line a large baking sheet with parchment paper and place the cod fillets on top. Sprinkle evenly with the Old Bay, ½ teaspoon of salt, ¼ teaspoon of pepper, and olive oil. Bake for 20 minutes or until just cooked through. Remove from the oven, let cool, and flake into small pieces with a fork.

5   Whisk the eggs gently in a small bowl. In a large bowl, combine the eggs, bell pepper, onion, parsley, flour, and salt and black pepper. Add the flaked cod and mashed potato and fold together with a rubber spatula to combine. Using a scant ⅓ cup to measure the mixture, form into patties on a large plate or baking sheet.

6   Refrigerate the patties for 30 minutes to firm them up and make them easier to pan-fry without falling apart.

7   **TO MAKE THE TARTAR SAUCE:** While you wait, in a small bowl, whisk together the mayonnaise, lemon juice, relish, mustard, capers, and black pepper. Refrigerate until ready to serve.

8 When ready to pan-fry, add 2 tablespoons of neutral oil to a large cast-iron pan set over medium-high heat. When shimmering hot, add several fish cakes—you'll need to cook them in a couple of batches to avoid overcrowding the pan. Cook for 3 to 4 minutes per side until golden. They need a nice crust to make flipping them easy. Add oil between batches if needed. Drain the cod cakes on a wire rack and then serve with tartar sauce alongside and a squeeze of lemon on top.

PASTA AL FORNO WITH BROCCOLI

MAKES 6 SERVINGS

Kosher salt

8 ounces brown rice penne or rigatoni pasta

2 heads broccoli, chopped into small florets (about 6 cups)

2 tablespoons extra-virgin olive oil

Freshly cracked black pepper

3 garlic cloves, minced

3 fresh sage leaves, minced

Zest of ½ lemon

⅔ cup grated mozzarella

⅓ cup finely grated Pecorino Romano

⅓ cup coarse panko-style bread crumbs

Let's call this a "streamlined" al forno recipe. Pasta al forno is a classic Italian baked pasta of which there are geographical variations, many of which require a bechamel and can be a bit laborious. Not this one. I use less cheese and bread crumbs than a typical pasta al forno, and extra flavor from broccoli, sage, and lemon. Two asks of you: don't skip the roasted broccoli step. Roasting allows it to reach browned flavor status that it won't get within the pasta bake. Also, please grate your own cheese. Pre-grated cheese has preservatives that simply don't allow it to melt into luscious, cheesy strings. That's what we want, isn't it?

1 Preheat the oven 425°F.

2 In a large pot of generously salted boiling water, cook the pasta two minutes shy of the package directions. Scoop out 1 cup of the pasta water and reserve for later. We want the pasta to be quite al dente since it's getting cooked again in the oven. Rinse the pasta with cool water to stop the cooking, then drain again and set aside.

3 On a large baking pan, toss the broccoli florets with 1 tablespoon of the olive oil, ½ teaspoon of salt, and a few cracks of pepper. Roast for about 20 minutes, until browned. Remove from the oven and immediately toss with the garlic, sage leaves, and lemon zest on the pan.

4 Spray an 11 by 7-inch baking dish with nonstick cooking oil.

5 Add the cooked pasta, ½ cup of the reserved pasta water, ½ teaspoon of salt, and the mozzarella. Toss. Add the broccoli mixture to the pan and toss again to combine.

6 If the mixture looks dry, add a bit more of the pasta water.

7 In a small bowl, toss together the Pecorino Romano, bread crumbs, and the remaining 1 tablespoon of olive oil. Top the pasta with the mixture. (The dish may be covered at this point and held at room temperature until ready to bake.)

8 Bake, uncovered, for about 20 minutes until the top is crisp and golden. Serve.

SIMPLEST ROAST CHICKEN *WITH* TARRAGON MUSTARD SAUCE

MAKES 4 SERVINGS

1   (3½-pound) whole chicken, patted dry

2½ teaspoons kosher salt

2   teaspoons freshly cracked black pepper

1   large onion, cut into eighths

1   tablespoon extra-virgin olive oil

TARRAGON MUSTARD SAUCE

1   medium shallot, minced

1   cup chicken stock (homemade or low-sodium)

2   tablespoons minced fresh tarragon

1   tablespoon Dijon mustard

3   tablespoons unsalted butter, cut into 3 pieces

    Kosher salt

    Freshly cracked black pepper

Knowing how to make a great roast chicken, with crispy skin and tender meat, is one of the foundations of a great home cook. This dish is at once rustic and elegant, reliable and exciting. The recipe isn't complicated—it just takes some planning, and I never tire of it. A few techniques make this chicken what it is: Refrigerating the salted chicken for a few hours, or ideally overnight, draws the moisture out of the skin and tenderizes the meat, making your chances of golden skin and luscious meat skyrocket. We don't oil or butter the chicken before cooking; we keep the chicken skin as dry as possible to brown. The trinity of tarragon, mustard, and butter in the sauce is as good a complement to roast chicken as I've ever tasted, but you can pair this roast chicken with a quick pan gravy, my Green Fridge Sauce (page 265), or nothing at all. It won't let you down.

1   Pat the chicken dry with paper towels and season it inside and out with the salt and pepper. If you have time, refrigerate the chicken, uncovered, overnight. If you're making it the day of, give it as much time as you can, at least a couple hours.

2   Bring the chicken to room temperature.

3   Stuff the cavity of the bird loosely with the onion pieces. You may not be able to fit them all. Tie the chicken legs together with kitchen twine to help the bird cook evenly.

4   Preheat the oven to 450°F and place a large cast-iron skillet (or heavy-bottomed roasting pan) in the oven to heat.

5   When the oven is at temperature, remove the pan and pour the olive oil in the bottom.

continues

6 Place the chicken on the pan breast-side up with the legs facing the back of the oven, where it's hottest. This will also help it cook evenly.

7 Roast for about 50 minutes, then baste with any pan juices. There won't be much. Continue roasting until the chicken's juices run clear when the skin is pierced with a knife and a thermometer registers 160° to 165°F, 5 to 10 minutes longer. Transfer the chicken to a large plate and tent with foil. Leave about 2 tablespoons of the fat in the skillet and discard the rest.

8 **TO MAKE THE TARRAGON MUSTARD SAUCE:** Heat the skillet from the chicken over medium-high heat. Sauté the shallot until softened, 1 to 2 minutes.

9 Add the chicken stock and tarragon and bring the heat to high, scraping the bottom of the pan as it boils. Continue to cook for 5 to 7 minutes until slightly thickened.

10 Whisk in the Dijon, then the butter and cook for 20 seconds more, whisking the whole time. Taste, and season with salt and pepper.

11 Serve the chicken with the sauce.

STICKY APRICOT-SOY OVEN-BAKED WINGS

MAKES 4 TO 6 SERVINGS

3 pounds chicken wings, wing tips removed and wings cut into 2 pieces

2 teaspoons kosher salt

2 tablespoons cornstarch

½ cup apricot preserves

1 tablespoon Worcestershire sauce

¼ cup soy sauce

1 tablespoon Dijon mustard

2 tablespoons apple cider vinegar

½ teaspoon freshly cracked black pepper

3 green onions, green parts only, sliced thin, for garnish

There is a delicious little restaurant nearby that makes Southeast Asian street food. Their pho and curry bowls are outstanding, and their tamarind wings almost upstage them all. These wings are inspired by those, and are pretty addictive for everyone who tastes them, including my children. After many tests, I found the best way to achieve a really crispy wing without frying is to toss them with cornstarch and bake them "naked" before saucing them to finish cooking. The sweet-sour-salty combination in the sauce is dynamite, and would be great with orange marmalade too. I like using Trader Joe's reduced-sugar apricot preserves in this glaze, but you can use any brand you like best.

1 Pat the wings dry.

2 In a large bowl, toss the wings in the salt and cornstarch to coat evenly.

3 Transfer the wings to a large rimmed baking sheet, leaving space between them to ensure proper air flow, and refrigerate, uncovered, for 2 hours. This helps to dehydrate the skin.

4 Preheat the oven to 450°F.

5 Remove the chicken tray from the refrigerator and place in the oven. Allow the wings to bake initially for 30 minutes.

6 Meanwhile, in a small saucepan set over medium heat, whisk together the apricot preserves, Worcestershire, soy sauce, Dijon, apple cider vinegar, 2 tablespoons of water, and the pepper. Cook for 3 to 5 minutes, whisking occasionally, until slightly thickened. Set aside.

7 Remove the chicken wings from the oven after their initial bake and brush them generously with some of the sauce. I like to pour about ½ cup into a separate bowl to avoid cross-contamination.

8 Return to the oven and finish cooking for 8 to 10 minutes until cooked through and a meat thermometer registers 165°F.

9 Remove from the oven and brush again with sauce, garnish with the green onions, and then serve right away with any extra sauce on the side.

SUNDAY MARINARA SAUCE

MAKES 4 CUPS ✳ A GENEROUS AMOUNT FOR 1 POUND OF PASTA

1   (28-ounce) can whole tomatoes, preferably San Marzano

2   tablespoons extra-virgin olive oil

1   small sweet onion, minced

2   garlic cloves, peeled and sliced thin

1   tablespoon tomato paste

1   teaspoon kosher salt

½   teaspoon dried oregano

⅛   teaspoon freshly cracked black pepper

My son, William, is the self-proclaimed sous chef of our house. This is one of the first recipes he asked to make with me, probably because he saw me using scissors to cut up the tomatoes and the chance to use "grown-up" scissors as a four-year-old boy was not one he would let pass him by. This recipe makes enough sauce for your pasta dinner with plenty of leftovers to freeze, meaning dinner is always just one step away on a busy weeknight. You won't find sugar in my marinara sauce; the gentle reduction of the tomatoes lends all the sweetness it needs. Feel free to double or triple this recipe and freeze the sauce in bags or freezer containers. This simple marinara sauce doesn't ask much of anything from you but time, and on Sunday we gladly make that time.

1   Remove the tomatoes from the cans and place in a large bowl, reserving their juices. Crush the tomatoes using your hands or a pair of kitchen scissors. Remove and discard the hard core from the stem ends, as well as any skin and tough membrane. Reserve.

2   Place the olive oil in a large saucepan over medium-low heat. Add the onion, and cook until soft and just beginning to brown, about 3 minutes. Stir in the garlic and cook until softened, about 30 seconds. Stir in the tomato paste and cook for 30 seconds to toast. Stir in the tomatoes and their reserved juices and add the salt and oregano. Increase the heat and bring to a boil. Immediately turn the heat to low, cover, and simmer until slightly thickened, about 1 hour, stirring every 15 minutes to prevent it from burning on the bottom.

3   Using an immersion blender, puree the sauce until smooth. Alternatively, you can mash the tomatoes with a potato masher for a chunkier sauce. Add the pepper, taste, and add salt if needed.

4   Continue cooking for 1 minute more. Remove from the heat and serve with pasta, or anything you like.

SMOKY SLOW-COOKED RIBS (AKA RUDY'S RIBS)

MAKES 4 SERVINGS

2 tablespoons kosher salt

½ teaspoon freshly cracked black pepper

1 teaspoon smoked paprika

2 tablespoons dark brown sugar

1 teaspoon dried oregano

1 teaspoon garlic powder

1 teaspoon onion powder

½ teaspoon ground coriander

2½ pounds baby back ribs

1 tablespoon extra-virgin olive oil

Many years ago, while living in Toronto, I spent a cold New Year's Eve with my dear friend and her family in Niagara-on-the-Lake in southern Ontario, Canada. Her mother and father, Jacqueline and Rudy, are excellent cooks, and we all made our contributions to the meal count. Rudy served a version of these ribs, and I remember wondering why I wasn't making ribs all year long. Over several hours they practically cook themselves, creating incredible smells in your kitchen. I took away many special things from that evening, including a sense of family that I was missing being so far from my own, and an indoor rib recipe that never lets me down.

1 Preheat the oven to 250°F.

2 In a small bowl, mix the salt, pepper, paprika, brown sugar, oregano, garlic powder, onion powder, and coriander with a fork. Set aside.

3 Cut two pieces of aluminum foil a few inches larger than a large baking sheet—one will go under and one will go over the ribs. Place one sheet on the pan and lay the ribs on top.

4 Drizzle the ribs with the olive oil and, using clean hands, rub the spice mixture all over the ribs. Get into every crevice. Lay the ribs meat-side up.

5 Place the second piece of foil on top of the ribs and crimp all around the sides to seal. Bake for 3½ to 4 hours until very tender and almost falling off the bone.

6 Remove from the oven and uncover the ribs. Turn the broiler to high. Broil the ribs for 5 to 7 minutes until well browned. Serve.

THE ULTIMATE BEEF MEATLOAF WITH CARAMELIZED ONIONS AND HORSERADISH

MAKES 8 SERVINGS

1 tablespoon extra-virgin olive oil

1 large onion, finely diced (about 2½ cups)

1 celery stalk, finely diced (about ⅓ cup)

3 garlic cloves, minced

Kosher salt

½ cup Fresh Bread Crumbs (page 260)

2 large eggs, beaten

1 tablespoon prepared horseradish

1 tablespoon Worcestershire sauce

¼ teaspoon freshly cracked black pepper

2 pounds ground beef (85% lean)

3 tablespoons good-quality ketchup

When there is meatloaf for dinner, the men in my life are happy. It's like it's in their genes. I've never met a man who didn't love meatloaf (when it's done right, that is).

I've taken a classic meatloaf recipe and added rich caramelized onions and bright horseradish to the mix. Cooking it with a pan of water in the oven keeps it light and tender—no heavy bricks of meatloaf for us. It's everything you love about the original, while feeling a bit special and modern at the same time. I guess that's kind of my thing.

1 Fill a baking dish with water and place on the lower third rack of the oven. This is going to help keep the meatloaf moist and prevent cracking.

2 Preheat the oven to 350°F.

3 In a medium skillet, heat the oil over medium-low heat. Cook the onion, stirring, for 20 minutes until caramelized. Add in the celery, garlic, and ¼ teaspoon of salt and cook for another 3 minutes until the vegetables are translucent. Remove from the heat and let cool to room temperature while you proceed.

4 In a large bowl, stir together the bread crumbs, eggs, horseradish, Worcestershire, 1½ teaspoons of salt, the pepper, and 1 tablespoon of water. Fold in the cooled vegetables. Add the beef and mix gently to combine. Shape the meatloaf into a 7 by 4-inch log and place on a foil-lined rimmed baking sheet. Brush all over with the ketchup.

5 Bake for 60 to 70 minutes until the internal temperature is 160°F and the meatloaf is cooked through.

6 Let the meatloaf rest, tented with foil, for 10 minutes before slicing it and serving hot. Leftovers make a delicious sandwich with some mayo on toasted sourdough bread.

VEGGIE-LOADED PEPPERS WITH QUINOA AND AGED CHEDDAR

MAKES 4 TO 6 SERVINGS

4   large yellow, orange, or red bell peppers, halved and cored, leaving the stems intact (if you wish)

3   tablespoons extra-virgin olive oil

Kosher salt

½   cup quinoa

1   small onion, finely diced

1   small zucchini, diced small

2   ears of corn, kernels removed

½   cup cherry tomatoes, quartered

Freshly cracked black pepper

⅛   teaspoon red pepper flakes (optional)

½   cup grated aged Cheddar cheese

½   cup finely chopped fresh basil and chives for garnish

These sunny, hearty stuffed peppers make me happy. I came up with them one summer night when I had a craving for stuffed . . . something . . . and wanted it to be lighter than a traditional meat-filled version.

The slight sweetness of the peppers and corn with the aged Cheddar and fluffy quinoa is delightful. We bake the peppers for a few minutes before stuffing, to tenderize them. I find baking them with liquid makes stuffed peppers too watery. Serve one or two halves per person, depending on what else you're having and how hungry you are. I bet you can guess how many I serve myself.

1   Preheat the oven to 450°F and line a baking sheet with parchment paper.

2   Place the peppers cut-side down on the sheet. Drizzle with 1 tablespoon of the olive oil and sprinkle with ½ teaspoon of salt. Transfer the pan to the oven and cook for 10 to 15 minutes, or until the peppers just begin to blister. Remove the peppers from the oven and turn them over. Set aside.

3   Fill a medium pot with water, salt it generously, and bring it to a simmer. Cook the quinoa for 9 to 12 minutes, or until it is just tender. Drain and set aside.

4   Meanwhile, heat the remaining 2 tablespoons of olive oil in a large skillet over medium heat. Add the onion and a pinch of salt. Cook, stirring, for about 5 minutes until the onion softens.

5   Add the zucchini and corn and cook for just 2 minutes. You don't want mushy zucchini—it's nice when it has some texture here. Turn off the heat and add the tomatoes and quinoa. Toss.

6   Stir, taste, and add salt, black pepper, and red pepper flakes if using.

7   Spoon a scant ½ cup of the filling generously into the cavity of each pepper and top with the Cheddar. Don't worry if the filling is spilling out of the peppers—we want peppers that

are packed *full*. If you are making ahead, you can cover the baking sheet with plastic wrap and refrigerate until you're ready to serve; just add on 5 to 10 minutes of baking time.

8 Cook the stuffed peppers for about 10 minutes until the cheese is melted and they are lightly browned.

9 Remove from the oven, top with the chives and basil, and serve.

BAKED STUFFED SHRIMP CASSEROLE

MAKES 4 SERVINGS

1 pound large shrimp, peeled with tails left intact, and deveined

1 tablespoon extra-virgin olive oil

Kosher salt

¼ teaspoon freshly cracked black pepper

1 pound lump crab meat

1 cup plain gluten-free cracker crumbs (such as Simple Mills)

2 garlic cloves, peeled and finely minced

⅓ cup chopped fresh parsley

Zest and juice of 1 lemon

6 tablespoons unsalted butter, melted

We didn't eat seafood all that much growing up—maybe because my father didn't love it—but we always had baked stuffed shrimp on Christmas Eve, and that inspired this recipe. My mom made it with Ritz crackers and lots of butter, and my mouth waters just thinking about it . . . I'm sure the excitement of opening presents after dinner aided in the enjoyment, but we just loved it. I suggest making this for any evening that you want to serve something special. It can easily be doubled for a dinner party or larger crowd. It tastes like a bit of a celebration to me.

1 Preheat the oven to 425°F.

2 Butterfly the shrimp by cutting down the back of the spine most of the way through, but not all the way. Add them to a medium bowl with the olive oil, ½ teaspoon of salt, and the pepper. Toss and set aside.

3 In a large bowl, make your stuffing by combining the crab meat, cracker crumbs, garlic, parsley, lemon zest and juice, melted butter, and ¼ teaspoon of salt.

4 In a 2-quart or an 11 by 17-inch oven-safe baking dish, arrange the seasoned shrimp evenly, cut-side down, so the tails are facing up.

5 Spoon the stuffing over and around the shrimp evenly.

6 Bake for 15 to 18 minutes until the shrimp is just cooked through and the top of the stuffing is golden brown. Serve with lemon wedges and a green salad.

THREE-YEAR GLUTEN-FREE BREAD

MAKES 1 ROUND BOULE-STYLE LOAF

1   cup white rice flour, plus more for dusting

½   cup oat flour

⅓   cup arrowroot starch

1   tablespoon potato starch

2½   teaspoons xanthan gum

1½   teaspoons instant yeast

1½   teaspoons kosher salt

1   teaspoon granulated sugar

1   teaspoon apple cider vinegar

1   egg white

Here it is, the bread you've all been waiting for. After two years of fielding requests for this recipe, I'm finally ready to put it in your hands. I knew I was saving it for this cookbook, but honestly, I was still perfecting it too. Amazing gluten-free bread is hard to come by for a reason.

In 2020, when it seemed everyone started baking bread, I decided I was going to master the best gluten-free bread you could possibly make at home. Not a bread that is "good for a gluten-free bread," but a bread so crusty, tender, and flavorful that no one would even know the difference. Three years later, I did just that.

I implore you to approach this recipe, and baking in general, really, with curiosity (especially when frustration starts to brew). There are many factors in a home baker's environment, from humidity in the air to the proportion of egg yolk to white in an egg, that affect your outcome, so give yourself a little time to practice and learn the nuances of what baking a loaf of bread looks like for you.

1   In the bowl of a standing mixer fitted with the paddle attachment, combine the white rice flour, oat flour, arrowroot starch, potato starch, xanthan gum, yeast, salt, and sugar and mix for 10 seconds on low.

2   In a large wet-ingredient measuring cup showing ounces, add the apple cider vinegar and egg white. Fill with enough warm water (95° to 100°F for maximum yeast blooming) to make 10 ounces of liquid.

3   Starting with the mixer set on low, add the liquid mixture to the dry ingredients and mix until a soft dough starts to form. It will slosh around in the liquid at first, but it will come together as you continue to blend.

4   Turn the mixer to medium-high and blend for 1 minute more.

5   The mixture should feel like soft biscuit dough, and may be wetter than you think it should be.

continues

6   With a rubber spatula, scoop the dough into the center of the bowl and smooth the top. Cover with a kitchen towel and leave it to rest in a warm place for an hour—one way to create the perfect warm spot is to turn your oven on to preheat for exactly one minute, then turn it off and put the bowl in. It won't rise much compared to a typical bread dough; this step is mostly for developing flavor.

7   Fit a Dutch oven with a piece of parchment paper large enough to go up the sides and cover them completely, then lay the paper on the counter. When the dough is finished resting, use a rubber spatula to scoop it onto the parchment paper. Have a small bowl of room-temperature water next to you, and gently shape the dough into a ball. Using a pretty soft touch, smooth the sides and top in a swooping motion, almost like you're making pottery. Upward diagonal motions will give the dough as much height as possible without knocking out the air that developed during the bread's resting time. Smooth out the exterior and any large air pockets. If any remain, the baked bread will still be delicious, but may look a bit lumpy.

8   Dust the top and sides with rice flour, then make 1 to 3 shallow cuts with a very sharp knife (or razor blade) about ¾ inch deep in the top of the loaf, such as one long and one short curved cut down the length of the bread, or two cut-cross patterns for a round boule like this.

9 Pick up the ends of the paper to transfer the dough in its paper sling to the Dutch oven. Cover with the lid and place in the middle of a cold oven.

10 Heat the oven to 425°F.

11 Bake for 75 to 85 minutes, until the bread is puffed up and golden. Take the lid off and bake for 20 to 25 minutes more. It should be nicely browned with a crisp crust that holds its shape when you press on it.

12 If you want to be absolutely sure the bread is done, insert an instant-read thermometer all the way to the bottom of the loaf (but not touching the pan). The temperature should be 205° to 210°F when it is done.

13 Remove the bread right away to a wire rack and let it rest for at least one hour, preferably two.

14 If gluten-free bread is cut into while it is still cooling, it will appear underdone and be gummy inside. It's hard to wait, but trust me on this one.

15 Slice and serve.

16 Leftover bread should be wrapped tightly and stored at room temperature for only 1 to 2 days. Any bread we don't eat by the next day, I freeze for morning toasts and sandwiches.

MODERN MAMA POT ROAST

MAKES 8 SERVINGS

¼ cup gluten-free all-purpose flour

Kosher salt

1 teaspoon freshly cracked black pepper

5 pounds rump of beef (or other roast suitable for slow cooking, such as chuck roast)

2 tablespoons neutral oil

2 onions, halved lengthwise and sliced into 1-inch half-moons

4 large carrots, peeled and cut into 2-inch pieces

2 dried bay leaves

6 sprigs thyme

1 cup chicken stock (homemade or low-sodium)

2 pounds Yukon Gold or red potatoes, cut into 2-inch pieces

Pot roast, to me, feels like home. I remember my mom making it for us on a cold winter's night and it was like comfort in a bowl. I still think it is. This one is incredibly flavorful, with meat that is perfectly seared for extra flavor and meltingly tender inside. With carrots, onions, and potatoes, it's a full meal and takes the guesswork out of dinner planning. I may have tweaked a couple of things from my mom's recipe—more vegetables, fresh herbs—but the essence of her pot roast is what I taste when I take my first bite.

1 Preheat the oven to 350°F.

2 On a small plate, combine the flour with 1 tablespoon of salt and the pepper and whisk together. Pat the flour firmly into the meat, covering all sides.

3 Heat a large Dutch oven over medium-high and add the oil.

4 Brown the meat on all sides for 4 to 6 minutes per side until deeply golden, then flip.

5 Add the onions, carrots, bay leaves, thyme, and stock. If your stock is unsalted, add a pinch of salt. Cover with a lid and transfer to the oven for 3 to 3½ hours until the meat is fork tender. During the last 20 to 25 minutes, remove from the oven and add the potatoes to cook.

6 Serve generous helpings in shallow bowls with crusty bread for sopping up the sauce.

SAFFRON RICE BAKE WITH CHICKPEAS, TOMATOES, AND LOADS OF GARLIC

MAKES 6 SERVINGS

2 cups cherry tomatoes

12 large garlic cloves, peeled and smashed

2 medium yellow onions, cut into half-moons

¼ teaspoon red pepper flakes

Kosher salt

3 tablespoons extra-virgin olive oil

1½ cups uncooked basmati rice, rinsed

1 (15-ounce) can chickpeas, drained and rinsed

Freshly cracked black pepper

½ teaspoon saffron threads

4 to 5 sprigs thyme

½ cup chopped fresh cilantro, parsley, or chives (or mix of any)

My husband likes my food. However, it's rather seldom that he makes a big deal about a dish that is vegan. Mind you, I didn't set out to make this baked rice vegan—it just inherently is. The particular day that I made this recipe, he came home late from work and heated some up while the kids and I got ready for bed. He made a point of telling me later, "That rice was incredible. It has so much flavor." That's when I knew I had to include it here. Saffron is expensive, but you don't need a lot, and the rest of this dish is so affordable that I suggest you allow yourself a little splurge. You'll be glad you did.

1 Preheat the oven to 325°F.

2 In a 9 by 13-inch casserole dish, toss together the tomatoes, garlic, onions, red pepper flakes, and ½ teaspoon of salt. Pour the olive oil over everything, then bake until the vegetables are soft, about an hour. Remove from the oven and raise the oven temperature to 450°F.

3 Give the vegetables a quick stir, then sprinkle the rice and chickpeas evenly over the vegetables. Top with 1½ teaspoons of salt, plenty of black pepper, the saffron, and the thyme sprigs. You'll remove the sprigs before serving.

4 Carefully pour 2½ cups of boiling water over the rice, then cover the dish tightly with foil and bake for 25 minutes or so until the rice is fluffy and the liquid is absorbed. Remove from the oven and set aside for 10 minutes, still covered.

5 Remove the foil, discard the thyme sprigs, and gently stir in the fresh herbs. Taste, and add more salt if needed, then serve.

*

VEGGIES

+

SIDES

ACTUALLY DELICIOUS BRAISED BROCCOLI

MAKES 4 SERVINGS

2 tablespoons extra-virgin olive oil

2 garlic cloves, minced

1 shallot, sliced thin

1½ pounds broccoli (2 large heads), cut into florets

1 cup low-sodium chicken or vegetable stock (or Scrappy Slow-Cooker Chicken Stock, page 165)

Kosher salt

My brother and I were those kids that cleaned our plates of broccoli and asked for more. It probably had something to do with the salty, savory chicken stock that my mom used to steam it. Broccoli takes really well to the braising method we use for meats, as it is a sure-fire way to build flavor. This is the way I make broccoli most often, and I now am the mother of those kids that like broccoli too.

1 Heat the olive oil in a large skillet over medium heat.

2 Add the garlic and shallot to the skillet and cook, stirring occasionally, for 3 to 5 minutes, or until the garlic and shallot soften and start to color. Add the broccoli and cook, stirring, for 3 to 4 minutes.

3 Add the stock and ½ to 1 teaspoon of salt depending on if the stock has salt in it. Cover and simmer for 3 to 5 minutes until the broccoli is tender. Serve.

CACIO E PEPE CAULIFLOWER

MAKES 4 SERVINGS

1   large head cauliflower, cut into small florets (8 cups)

2   tablespoons unsalted butter, melted

1   garlic clove, finely minced

½   teaspoon kosher salt

½   teaspoon freshly cracked black pepper

5   tablespoons Pecorino Romano, divided

Cacio e pepe, translating to "cheese and pepper" in Italian, is one of my very favorite pastas in the world. Here we borrow the simple, pungent magic from sharp cheese, just enough butter, and lots of black pepper to smother small bits of cauliflower before and after they hit the oven. Maybe you've never stood over the counter risking burnt fingers to tuck into a tray of hot, crispy, cheesy cauliflower, but you will when you make this.

1   Preheat the oven to 425°F.

2   Line two baking sheets with parchment paper. Divide the florets evenly between the two, being careful not to overcrowd the pans.

3   Drizzle the butter over the florets, then toss them well so all of them are covered. Sprinkle with the garlic, salt, pepper, and 3 tablespoons of the Pecorino Romano. Toss. Don't worry if a lot of cheese falls off, it will crisp up and get delicious on the paper. Make sure the cauliflower is spread evenly.

4   Roast for 10 minutes, give it a toss, then return to the oven for another 10 minutes, or until the cauliflower is golden and roasted and the cheese is crisp on the paper. Remove the pan from the oven and sprinkle immediately with the remaining 2 tablespoons of Pecorino Romano. Let sit for 2 to 3 minutes before transferring to a platter. Serve.

GARLICKY GREEN BEANS WITH HAZELNUTS AND THYME

MAKES 4 SERVINGS

Kosher salt

⅓ cup raw hazelnuts

16 ounces (2 cups) green beans, stemmed

1 tablespoon unsalted butter

2 garlic cloves, minced

1 tablespoon minced fresh thyme

Freshly cracked black pepper

If I'm asking you to prepare an ice bath, it's for a reason. The blanch-and-sauté method retains the snap of the green beans and preserves their color, because no one deserves mushy green beans. Don't feel like getting hazelnuts? Use almonds instead—they're a classic accompaniment to green beans. If you're serving this for a dinner party or holiday, and I suggest you do, you can make most of it ahead and sauté in just minutes before serving.

1 Fill a large pot with 4 quarts of water, add 1 tablespoon of salt, and bring to a boil.

2 While the water comes to a boil, place the hazelnuts in a medium sauté pan and set over medium heat. Cook them for 5 to 7 minutes, shaking the pan occasionally, until they start to darken and smell nutty. Transfer to a clean kitchen towel. Fold the towel over the nuts and roll them around until some of the skins fall off. They won't all come off—it's all good. Coarsely chop the hazelnuts and set aside. Wipe the pan out with the towel.

3 When the water has come to a boil, add the green beans and cook for 1 minute until slightly tender. Drain and transfer them to a large bowl of ice water. Set aside.

4 Melt the butter in the sauté pan over medium heat. Add the garlic and cook for 30 seconds, stirring constantly, until lightly browned. Using a slotted spoon, add the green beans to the pan. Add the thyme, 1 teaspoon of salt, and ¼ teaspoon of pepper and cook for 3 to 5 minutes, stirring with tongs, until heated through. Remove from the heat, stir in the chopped hazelnuts, and taste for seasonings. Serve warm or at room temperature.

SPICY ASIAN CUCUMBERS

MAKES 4 TO 6 SERVINGS

2 English cucumbers

¼ teaspoon kosher salt

2 tablespoons soy sauce

3 tablespoons rice wine vinegar

1 teaspoon coconut sugar

2 garlic cloves, peeled and minced

2 tablespoons toasted sesame oil

¼ teaspoon red pepper flakes

This almost traditional cucumber salad uses all of my favorite Asian flavors to pack a serious umami flavor punch. You'll often find sugar or honey used in this classic recipe—I use coconut sugar because I like the deep caramel flavor to offset the heat. This is best after it sits in the fridge for a few hours, making it perfect for meal prep through the week. These salty, spicy cucumbers are excellent paired with salmon or shrimp or eaten right out of the bowl . . . most often my delivery method of choice.

1 Gently smash the cucumbers with the back of a heavy knife to just crack open. Chop into irregular 2-inch pieces and place in a medium bowl; sprinkle with the salt. Let the salted cucumbers sit while you make the dressing.

2 In a medium bowl, whisk together the soy sauce, vinegar, coconut sugar, and garlic. Set aside.

3 In a small saucepan, heat the sesame oil with the red pepper flakes until it starts to bubble. While very hot, add it to the marinade mixture.

4 Pat the cucumbers dry, discarding any liquid they have released, and add them to the bowl with dressing. Toss to coat evenly.

5 Place the cucumber salad in the refrigerator for at least an hour. The more time you give it, the more flavorful it will be. Serve.

CHARRED ASPARAGUS WITH CAPER-RAISIN RELISH

MAKES 6 SERVINGS

2   pounds thick asparagus (about 2 bunches)

Extra-virgin olive oil

1   tablespoon balsamic vinegar

2   tablespoons coarsely chopped (drained and rinsed) capers

¼   cup golden raisins

2   tablespoons finely chopped fresh parsley

¾   teaspoon kosher salt

Freshly cracked black pepper

¼   cup toasted pine nuts

My whole family loves asparagus, and truth be told I usually keep it simple with a quick roast of olive oil, salt, pepper, and finished with lemon because . . . children.

Capers and raisins combine here to make a quick, chunky vinaigrette that is salty-sweet and packed with flavor. Pine nuts add crunch, and are a pretty final touch. If your children haven't quite made it into caper territory yet either, simply serve the asparagus undressed for them and keep more of the slurpable relish for yourself.

1   Rinse the asparagus and pat it dry. Cut off the woody ends and discard.

2   To make the relish, combine 3 tablespoons of olive oil with the balsamic, capers, raisins, and parsley. Season the dressing to taste with ¼ teaspoon of the salt and a pinch of pepper. Set aside.

3   Preheat the broiler to high and insert a large, heavy rimmed baking sheet. This will heat up as the oven does, so the asparagus will start cooking immediately when it hits the pan.

4   Add the asparagus, 1 teaspoon of olive oil, the remaining ½ teaspoon of salt, and ¼ teaspoon of pepper to a large bowl and toss. Transfer the asparagus to the hot pan, reserving the bowl, and broil until tender and well charred, shaking occasionally, 4 to 8 minutes total. Place the charred asparagus on a serving platter and drizzle the relish over the top. Scatter with the toasted pine nuts and serve warm or at room temperature.

CRUNCHY, SALTY, HERBY AVOCADO WEDGES

MAKES 4 SERVINGS

2 cups coarsely chopped mixed fresh herbs (such as cilantro, mint, basil, and parsley)

2 ripe avocados

Juice of 1 lime

½ small red onion, finely minced

2 teaspoons extra-virgin olive oil

¼ teaspoon smoked paprika

⅓ cup toasted pumpkin seeds

Flaky sea salt

It's easy to overlook avocados as a side dish in and of themselves. They are capable of a lot more than guacamole and taco toppings, like in these insanely delicious avocado wedges nestled on fresh herbs and showered with lime juice, spices, and crisp pumpkin seeds. Serve this five-minute side with pan-fried salmon, grilled meats, and, yes, tacos. There's just no escaping the sense that would make.

1 On a medium serving platter, lay down 1 cup of the fresh herbs as a bed for the avocados. Halve the avocados, remove the pit with the heel of a knife, and peel off the skin with your hands. Place the avocado halves cut-side down on a cutting board and slice into ½-inch wedges.

2 Lay half of the avocado wedges on the herbs and top with half of the lime juice, onion, olive oil, paprika, and pumpkin seeds and a large sprinkle of salt.

3 Repeat the layer with the remaining ingredients, finishing with the pumpkin seeds and salt to taste, and serve right away.

FARRO WITH TOMATOES, SUMMER SQUASH, AND PARMESAN

MAKES 4 SERVINGS

2 cups pearled farro

Kosher salt

3 tablespoons extra-virgin olive oil

3 garlic cloves, thinly sliced

1 small yellow onion, diced finely

3 cups chopped (¾-inch cubes) yellow squash or zucchini (about 1 medium)

2 medium tomatoes, diced small (about 2 cups)

Balsamic vinegar

¼ teaspoon freshly cracked black pepper

½ cup minced fresh basil leaves

½ cup freshly grated Parmesan cheese

Chewy, nutty farro gets the risotto treatment: Farro is an ancient Italian grain that is earthier and heartier than rice, and doesn't release starch as it cooks, so this doesn't require constant tending to like risotto does. Be sure to use pearled farro, the easiest kind to find in most grocery stores, as the husks have been removed and it cooks in 10 to 15 minutes. Once you have this dish in your repertoire, you always have a starch-and-vegetable-in-one recipe, making getting a full dinner on the table a breeze. If you're vegetarian, serve a generous helping for dinner with or without a salad and call it a day.

1 Rinse the farro with cool water in a colander.

2 Bring a large pot of generously salted water to a boil. Add the farro and cook until tender according to package directions. Drain and let cool in the colander.

3 Heat 2 tablespoons of the olive oil in a large, heavy skillet over medium-high heat. Add the garlic and onion and sauté, stirring, for 2 minutes. Add the squash and cook for 5 to 7 minutes until it just starts to brown. Turn the heat to low, then add in the tomatoes and ½ teaspoon of salt. Continue to cook for 5 minutes, stirring occasionally, or until everything is tender but not mushy. Add in the balsamic, pepper, basil, cooked farro, and ¼ cup of the Parmesan and toss, then cook for 30 seconds more. Taste, and add a pinch of salt if needed.

4 Mound the farro mixture on four plates. While hot, top it with the remaining ¼ cup of the Parmesan. Drizzle with the remaining 1 tablespoon of olive oil and serve.

HARVEST VEGETABLE ROAST WITH PEARS

MAKES 6 TO 8 SERVINGS

1½ pounds parsnips (3 to 4), halved lengthwise and cut into 3-inch pieces

1½ pounds delicata squash, cut into 3-inch pieces

1 fennel bulb, halved and sliced ½ inch thick

1 pear, halved and cut into ½-inch wedges

10 shallots, sliced in half

10 sprigs total of thyme and rosemary, plus more for garnish

Cloves from 1 head garlic, unpeeled

¼ cup extra-virgin olive oil

¼ cup balsamic vinegar

¼ teaspoon ground nutmeg

Kosher salt

Freshly cracked black pepper

This recipe is a no-brainer for your Thanksgiving table, but is certainly not reserved for it. The idea of adding pear to the mix might seem odd, but it won't for long. The pear, along with balsamic vinegar, nutmeg, and lots of herbs, is what makes this stand out from the usual autumnal veggie roast. It's an excellent side for roasted chicken, or any roasted meat, and leftovers are delicious spooned onto some hearty greens with a simple vinaigrette.

1 Preheat the oven to 450°F. Set aside two large baking sheets.

2 In a large bowl, combine the parsnips, squash, fennel, pear, shallots, thyme and rosemary, and garlic. Add the olive oil, balsamic, nutmeg, 1 teaspoon of salt, and ¼ teaspoon of pepper and mix thoroughly with your hands.

3 Divide the vegetables between the two sheet pans and spread in an even layer, being sure there is room between the ingredients so that they brown instead of steam.

4 Roast for 40 to 45 minutes until golden and soft, tossing the vegetables and rotating the pans from top to bottom halfway through.

5 Remove from the oven and discard the herb sprigs. Squeeze the roasted garlic out of the skins and discard the skins, then add the garlic back to the vegetables.

6 Taste, add salt if needed, and serve.

HASHED BRUSSELS SPROUTS WITH GARLIC AND CITRUS

MAKES 4 SERVINGS

1 pound brussels sprouts, washed

2 tablespoons extra-virgin olive oil

½ large red onion, diced (¾ cup)

3 garlic cloves, minced

Kosher salt

Freshly cracked black pepper

1 tablespoon orange zest

3 tablespoons orange juice

⅓ cup chopped fresh parsley for serving

When it comes to brussels sprouts, once you hash, you never go back. These brussels sprouts are inspired by the hashed brussels sprouts that the late Union Square Café in New York City served, and they are one of my favorite ways to make this underrated cruciferous vegetable. I'm all for a good high roast with rich flavors during the winter months, but come spring and summer I want a brighter experience, and this is just that. Garlic, orange, and parsley make for a soft and refreshing combination, perfect for serving with grilled fish, pork, or chicken.

1 Using a mandoline or very sharp knife, slice the brussels sprouts to a ⅛-inch thickness. They will be all different shapes and sizes, and that's fine.

2 Heat the olive oil in a large sauté pan over medium-low heat.

3 Once the oil is warm, add the onion and cook for 5 minutes. Add the garlic with ¼ teaspoon of salt and cook for 2 to 3 minutes more, until softened and lightly golden.

4 Add the brussels sprouts along with 1 teaspoon of salt and a few cracks of black pepper and toss to coat.

5 Turn the heat to medium-high, add the orange zest and juice, and cook, stirring, for 3 to 5 minutes until just softened with browned edges.

6 Top the whole pan with the parsley and spoon onto a large platter. Enjoy!

HONEY HARISSA CARROTS WITH LABNEH

MAKES 4 SERVINGS

1	tablespoon honey
2	teaspoons harissa
1	tablespoon lemon juice
1½	pounds carrots, scrubbed or peeled, halved lengthwise and cut into 4-inch pieces
1	garlic clove, finely grated
2	tablespoons extra-virgin olive oil
1	teaspoon ground cumin
1	teaspoon kosher salt
¼	teaspoon freshly cracked black pepper
1	cup labneh
1	tablespoon minced fresh cilantro

When I tell you that the first time I made this recipe, I sat down and ate the entire platter for dinner, I'm not exaggerating. One and a half pounds of carrots, down the hatch.

Harissa and labneh are two ingredients you may not be familiar with, but don't let that deter you, as most grocery stores carry both: harissa is a hot North African chili paste that is mixed with honey and spices, used here to glaze the carrots, and labneh is a dense strained yogurt with the consistency of cream cheese, which offers a cooling refuge for the spiced carrots in this recipe. If you don't want to seek either out, however, use your favorite chili paste or sauce (sriracha works) and a good full-fat Greek yogurt. It'll be delicious, I assure you.

1. Preheat the oven to 450°F.

2. In a small bowl, whisk the honey, harissa, and lemon juice to combine. Set aside.

3. On a large sheet pan, toss the carrots with the garlic, olive oil, cumin, salt, and pepper. Arrange them in a flat layer with a bit of space in between the pieces.

4. Roast, tossing occasionally, until tender and caramelized, 20 to 25 minutes.

5. When the carrots come out of the oven, toss them quickly with the harissa mixture and let them cool to room temperature.

6. Add the labneh to a shallow platter or evenly divide onto serving plates. Smear it in a single layer, using a swirling motion with the back of a large spoon.

7. Pile the carrots on top, finish with the cilantro, and serve.

PARMESAN ROASTED ZUCCHINI

MAKES 6 SERVINGS

4   small zucchini (about 2 pounds)

⅓   cup freshly grated Parmesan cheese

1   teaspoon garlic powder

1   teaspoon onion powder

½   teaspoon paprika

1   teaspoon kosher salt

¼   teaspoon freshly cracked black pepper

2   tablespoons extra-virgin olive oil

I admit it: I came up with this recipe as a way to get my kids to eat zucchini. It worked. Zucchini can be a tricky vegetable to get right on its own, so I understand the apprehension—it seems to get mushy the moment it hits heat due to its high water content, making it quite easy to overcook. Here I call for small zucchini, because they have a lower water content than large, so find the smallest you can. By cutting the zucchini into large wedges and coating them with spiced Parmesan cheese, we slow down the cooking process, giving the inside time to tenderize and the crust time to develop. Roasting the zucchini on a rack also means it doesn't sit in any juices that escape, but instead gets a nice blast of heat from all sides. Kid and adult approved.

1   Preheat the oven to 425°F.

2   Trim the ends off the zucchini and quarter them lengthwise. Cut each spear in half so that you have eight 3- to 4-inch pieces.

3   Coat a wire rack with nonstick spray and place it on a large rimmed baking sheet. Pat the zucchini wedges dry.

4   In a small bowl, mix the Parmesan, garlic powder, onion powder, paprika, salt, and pepper.

5   Place the zucchini in a large bowl. Drizzle with the olive oil and sprinkle with the Parmesan mixture. Toss to coat, then arrange the zucchini on top of the wire rack on the baking sheet, avoiding overlap as much as possible.

6   Place in the oven and bake until the zucchini is just tender, 9 to 12 minutes depending on the size.

7   Turn the broiler on high. Cook until the Parmesan is lightly crisp, 3 to 4 minutes, rotating the tray as needed. Keep a close eye on them so they don't burn.

8   Serve warm.

QUICK MARINATED VEGETABLES WITH BALSAMIC AND HERBS

MAKES 4 TO 6 SERVINGS

1 medium eggplant, sliced on a long diagonal into ½-inch pieces

2 medium zucchini, sliced on a long diagonal into ½-inch-thick pieces

2 orange or red bell peppers, seeded and quartered

2 small red onions, quartered into wedges

⅓ cup extra-virgin olive oil

2 tablespoons balsamic vinegar

2 large garlic cloves, minced

2 teaspoons kosher salt

⅛ teaspoon freshly cracked pepper

¼ cup chopped mixed fresh herbs (such as parsley, basil, thyme, and oregano)

I learned to make these marinated vegetables in culinary school. I know what you're thinking: "You needed to go to culinary school to grill vegetables?" Apparently I did. These weren't like any grilled vegetable I'd had before—they were flavored inside and out, and I couldn't stop eating them. They were also incredibly simple to make, with all the prep done ahead of time, and they go with just about anything from grilled meats and fish to pasta, making these vegetables a perfect side dish for a barbecue. This quick marinade, done while you're heating the grill essentially, can certainly be made early in the day and stored in the refrigerator. I make these all summer long, with all sorts of vegetables, but this is my go-to combination.

1 In a large bowl, combine the eggplant, zucchini, bell peppers, onions, olive oil, balsamic, garlic, salt, pepper, and mixed herbs. Toss well to combine and let the vegetables hang out at room temperature while you turn on the grill.

2 Heat a grill or grill pan to medium-high heat. If you're using a grill pan, you will grill these in two batches.

3 Remove the vegetables and place them onto skewers for easy maneuvering, or directly onto the grill. Reserve the leftover marinade. Grill until tender and lightly charred all over, 6 to 10 minutes. Resist moving them around too much, and flip just once if those pronounced grill marks are what you are after. When done, toss the vegetables back in the bowl of marinade once more to coat, and serve warm or at room temperature.

PROVENÇAL BAKED TOMATOES

MAKES 4 TO 8 SERVINGS

4 tablespoons extra-virgin olive oil

4 large, firm tomatoes

¾ cup Fresh Bread Crumbs (page 260), dried, or panko-style bread crumbs

1 large garlic clove, grated

½ teaspoon herbes de Provence

3 tablespoons minced fresh parsley

2 tablespoons minced fresh basil

Kosher salt

¼ teaspoon freshly cracked black pepper

4 tablespoons grated Gruyère cheese

My mother made a teriyaki steak we all loved growing up, and stuffed tomatoes usually sat alongside. This is how I like to make stuffed tomatoes, inspired by her, and I also often serve them with steak (I come by it honestly). It's one of the only ways I will eat fresh tomatoes in the winter, as this savory stuffed preparation can transform a sad off-season tomato.

Of course, in-season tomatoes make this dish even better. You can wrap them in foil and throw them on the grill in the summer if it is already going. This one's a keeper.

1 Preheat the oven to 400°F.

2 Brush a 9 by 13-inch baking dish with 1 tablespoon of the olive oil.

3 Remove the stems from the tomatoes, then cut them in half crosswise through the equator of the tomato.

4 With your fingers or a teaspoon, remove the seeds and juice. Place the halves upside down on a paper towel to drain while you make the filling.

5 In a small bowl, combine the bread crumbs, garlic, herbes de Provence, 2 tablespoons of the parsley, the basil, ½ teaspoon of salt, ⅛ teaspoon of the pepper, and 2 tablespoons of the Gruyère.

6 Drizzle 1 tablespoon of the olive oil into the bowl and stir again to combine.

7 Pat the tomato halves dry and place them cut-side up in the baking dish. Sprinkle each half with a pinch of salt.

8 Divide the filling evenly among the tomato halves, then press down slightly on the filling. Sprinkle the remaining 2 tablespoons of Gruyère over the tomatoes and drizzle with the remaining 2 tablespoons of olive oil.

9 Bake until the filling is golden brown and the tomatoes just start to split, about 35 minutes. Serve hot or at room temperature, topped with the remaining 1 tablespoon of parsley.

SALT AND VINEGAR SMASHED POTATOES

MAKES 6 TO 8 SERVINGS

2 pounds small, waxy potatoes (new potatoes or fingerlings are great)

2 cups white wine vinegar

Kosher salt

½ cup extra-virgin olive oil

2 garlic cloves, minced fine

¼ teaspoon freshly cracked black pepper

¼ cup chives, minced

Salt and vinegar potato chips are elite, and they are the inspiration for these easy smashed potatoes. We parboil the potatoes in vinegar and water to flavor them throughout before a roast in the oven takes over. With only a handful of ingredients, you have a potato that's creamy inside and crispy outside with salty, punchy flavor. Serve with a nice steak and green salad for a simple home-run dinner.

1 Preheat the oven to 450°F.

2 Place the whole potatoes in a large pot along with the vinegar. Add water to cover, along with a large pinch of salt and bring to a boil. Lower the heat and let simmer, cooking the potatoes until they are easily pierced with a fork but still holding together, 12 to 20 minutes depending on size. Drain the potatoes in a colander.

3 Brush 1 tablespoon of the oil each on the bottom of two large rimmed baking sheets and place the potatoes on top. Using the bottom of a glass, smash each potato until it is flattened. Drizzle the rest of the olive oil on top and sprinkle with the garlic, 1 teaspoon of salt, and the pepper.

4 Roast the potatoes until they are browned and very crispy, about 30 minutes. Serve topped with the chives.

SWEET POTATOES AGRODOLCE

MAKES 4 TO 6 SERVINGS

2 pounds orange sweet potatoes (3 to 4), peeled and sliced into ¼-inch-thick rounds

¼ cup extra-virgin olive oil

3 tablespoons honey

½ teaspoon kosher salt

¼ teaspoon freshly cracked black pepper

¼ cup apple cider vinegar

1 jalapeño or Fresno chile, seeded and thinly sliced into rings

1 garlic clove, thinly sliced

3 to 4 fresh sage leaves, thinly sliced

¼ cup pumpkin seeds, toasted

I came up with this recipe one November evening when I was thinking of new ways to make sweet potatoes for Thanksgiving. I wanted something universally delicious with history to it, but that also felt modern. I'd venture to say you could toss this traditional Sicilian sauce on any vegetable and it would be fabulous. "Agrodolce" quite literally means "sweet and sour" in Italian. Adding chili pepper for spice, sage for herbaceous warmth, and pumpkin seeds for crunch takes these easy sweet potatoes to a whole new level. It's also quite beautiful—glossy and elegant—which never hurts. Serve this for Thanksgiving, and for a side with dinner any fall or winter evening.

1 Preheat the oven to 425°F and line two large rimmed baking sheets with parchment paper.

2 Place the sweet potatoes in a large bowl and drizzle them with the oil and 1 tablespoon of the honey, and sprinkle with the salt and pepper. Toss to coat evenly.

3 Transfer the potatoes to the baking sheets and spread them out evenly.

4 Roast the potatoes until caramelized, 20 to 25 minutes, flipping the potatoes and rotating the pans halfway through.

5 Meanwhile, in a small saucepan, bring the apple cider vinegar, jalapeño, garlic, and the remaining 2 tablespoons of honey to a boil over medium heat. Turn the heat to low and simmer for 5 to 7 minutes until the mixture coats the back of a spoon.

6 When the potatoes are finished, arrange them on a shallow platter and spoon the agrodolce sauce over them.

7 Top with the sage leaves and pumpkin seeds and serve right away.

DESSERT MENU

THREE-INGREDIENT MANGO SORBET

MAKES 4 TO 5 SERVINGS

3 cups frozen mango

1 (13.5-ounce) can full-fat coconut milk

¼ cup honey

⅛ teaspoon kosher salt

Flaky sea salt for serving (optional)

Three ingredients, an ice cube tray, and a blender. That's all you need for this lovely, creamy sorbet that caters to everyone. It's refreshing and rich with the soft pucker of mango, not like those icy, sugar-coma-inducing sorbets of the past. It's the perfect palate-cleansing dessert for a summer dinner party and any hot evening. You can make the ice cubes ahead and simply blitz in the blender five minutes before you want to serve it.

1 In a high-speed blender, combine the mango, coconut milk, honey, and kosher salt. Process on high until very smooth, using a tamper as needed to keep things moving.

2 Use a small measuring cup or large spoon to pour the mixture into ice cube trays, filling the cavities about three-quarters full.

3 Freeze the cubes for at least 4 hours until solid. If you are making ahead, pop the cubes out into a freezer-safe bag (Ziplock or other) and freeze for up to 2 weeks until ready to serve the sorbet.

4 To make the sorbet, transfer the frozen cubes back to a high-speed blender and pulse to chop. When the bits are small, turn up the machine and process until it's the texture of soft-serve ice cream, scraping the sides of the bowl as needed.

5 Scoop the sorbet into small serving bowls and serve with a sprinkle of flaky sea salt, if desired.

ALMOND CARDAMOM CAKE

MAKES ONE 8-INCH ROUND CAKE

1¾ cups gluten-free all-purpose flour

½ cup almond flour

1 cup granulated sugar

1½ teaspoons kosher salt

½ teaspoon baking soda

¾ teaspoon baking powder

1 teaspoon ground cardamom

⅔ cup neutral oil

1¼ cups unsweetened almond milk

3 large eggs

1 teaspoon vanilla extract

Zest of 1 lemon

GLAZE

Juice of 1 lemon

4 tablespoons confectioners' sugar

½ teaspoon almond extract

⅛ teaspoon kosher salt

½ cup sliced toasted almonds

I hate to pick favorite children, but this cake has my heart. It's somewhere between a French almond cake and an Italian olive oil cake, with a devastatingly moist crumb infused with cardamom. The simple citrus almond glaze that is brushed on after baking will rescue a slightly overbaked cake and brings a perfectly baked cake to luscious glory. It's also rather beautiful, and will leave guests *ooh*ing and *aah*ing.

There are a handful of recipes in this book that made me immediately call my mother after the first time I tasted them. This is one.

1 Preheat the oven to 350°F.

2 Spray an 8-inch round cake pan (that is at least 2 inches deep) with nonstick cooking spray and line the bottom with parchment paper. Set aside.

3 In a medium bowl, whisk together the all-purpose flour, almond flour, granulated sugar, salt, baking soda, baking powder, and cardamom. In another large bowl, whisk together the oil, almond milk, eggs, vanilla, and lemon zest. Reserve the zested lemon to be used in the glaze.

4 Add the dry ingredients to the wet ingredients and whisk just until there are no more traces of flour.

5 Pour the batter into the prepared pan and bake for 70 to 75 minutes until the top is golden and a cake tester comes out just clean.

6 **WHILE THE CAKE BAKES, MAKE THE GLAZE:** Combine the lemon juice, 2 tablespoons of the confectioners' sugar, the almond extract, and salt in a small bowl. Stir with a whisk until smooth. Cover and set aside.

7 When the cake is baked, let cool in the pan for 15 minutes before running a knife around the edge of the pan and inverting the cake onto a wire rack. While the cake is still warm, use a pastry brush to gently pat the glaze all over the cake. Just keep going over the cake until the glaze is gone. Some of it will drip off, but most of it will soak in. Sprinkle the toasted almonds over the top of the cake while the glaze is wet, and pat gently. Allow the cake to cool completely, then sprinkle with the remaining 2 tablespoons of confectioners' sugar and serve.

APPLE THYME TORTE

MAKES ONE 9-INCH ROUND TORTE

2   medium Granny Smith apples

⅔   cup granulated sugar

½   cup coconut oil, room temperature

2   large eggs, room temperature

1   teaspoon vanilla extract

1¼   cups gluten-free all-purpose flour

1½   teaspoons baking powder

½   teaspoon kosher salt

½   teaspoon chopped fresh thyme leaves

1   tablespoon Demerara or cane sugar

Coconut whipped cream (or regular) for serving

This torte is so easy to make, you could bake it every week. When you taste it, you might just want to do that. A torte by definition is a rich cake originating in Austria, and can be multilayered and frosted or filled with fruit as you see here. The batter calls for a small amount of flour compared to other ingredients, and it will seem as though there isn't enough of it as you mix in the apples. Have faith: the torte transforms itself as it bakes, billowing up around the apples and then sinking back down to result in a rustic, condensed cake whose flavor can't be beat. Don't balk at the thyme in this recipe—it's just that little hint of something in the background that warms up the flavor.

1   Preheat the oven to 350°F.

2   Spray a 9-inch springform pan with nonstick cooking spray and set aside.

3   Peel the apples and cut them into about a 1-inch dice. Reserve.

4   In the bowl of a stand mixer, beat the granulated sugar and coconut oil for 1 minute until fluffy. Add the eggs and vanilla and mix for 20 seconds to combine well.

5   Add the flour, baking powder, salt, and thyme and mix with the paddle attachment for 10 seconds until it is combined.

6   Remove the bowl from the mixer, add the apples to it, and fold them in by hand.

7   Pour the batter into the prepared pan and smooth the top.

8   Sprinkle the top with the Demerara sugar and bake for 45 to 50 minutes until the top is golden and the cake is cooked through.

9   Let the cake cool in the pan on a wire rack before unmolding. Serve with whipped cream.

BROWN BUTTER BRICKLE BARS

MAKES SIXTEEN 2-INCH SQUARES

3   Heath bars (about 4.5 ounces if using toffee bits)

6   cups gluten-free crispy rice cereal

5   tablespoons unsalted butter

½   teaspoon kosher salt

½   teaspoon vanilla extract

1   (10-ounce) bag marshmallows

These are like grown-up Rice Krispies Treats, with a deep caramel flavor throughout due to both browned butter and chunks of toffee. When I need to come up with a dessert fast for a casual get-together, I make these and they never disappoint. Heath bars just make everything better—even Rice Krispies Treats, which are pretty hard to improve upon. Note that if you use that main brand of crispy rice cereal, they are not technically gluten-free since they contain malt syrup derived from barley. For anyone sensitive to gluten, pick up one of the many brands of crispy rice cereal that are gluten-free.

1   Spray an 8-inch square baking dish with nonstick cooking spray and set aside.

2   **IF YOU'RE USING TOFFEE BITS, SKIP THIS STEP:** Place the Heath bars in a large plastic bag and smash them gently a few times with a meat cleaver or rolling pin to break up the pieces into small bits.

3   Place the cereal in a large bowl and set aside.

4   In a small saucepan over medium-low heat, melt the butter. Stir it continuously until it has developed a golden color and a nutty aroma, 4 to 6 minutes. Add the salt and vanilla and stir once. Quickly add the marshmallows and cook on low heat, stirring, until they are totally melted into the butter, 3 to 4 minutes.

5   Pour the marshmallow mixture into the bowl with the cereal and stir briefly. Add half of the toffee bits and stir once more.

6   Immediately transfer the mixture into the prepared baking dish and gently pat it in and smooth the top. Don't pat down with force, as we don't want them too dense—we like them high and fluffy. Add the remainder of the toffee bits evenly on top. Set aside to cool for at least 30 minutes.

7   Slice into squares and serve.

COCONUT CORNFLAKE COOKIES

MAKES 16 TO 18 COOKIES

½ cup coconut oil, room temperature

⅔ cup granulated sugar

2 large eggs, room temperature

2 teaspoons vanilla extract

1 cup gluten-free all-purpose flour

½ teaspoon kosher salt

1 teaspoon baking soda

¼ teaspoon ground cinnamon

1 cup old-fashioned rolled oats

1¼ cups cornflakes cereal

1 cup unsweetened shredded coconut

This cookie is very loosely inspired by the Cornflake Marshmallow Cookies, one of my favorite treats from Momofuku Milk Bar, the über-talented Christina Tosi's brainchild. I made these cookies one Fourth of July afternoon before heading to a party at the beach. Chilling the scooped cookie dough concentrates the flavor and prevents the fat from spreading too much in the oven, resulting in evenly baked, uniform cookies. The double dose of coconut oil and shredded coconut gives them a pronounced flavor I'm always looking for in coconut desserts but seldom find. They are crispy and golden with a chewy center, and positively addictive.

1 In a large bowl, using a stand or handheld mixer, cream together the coconut oil and sugar for 2 minutes until well combined and lighter in texture.

2 Add the eggs and vanilla and mix for another 20 seconds to incorporate, scraping the sides of the bowl with a spatula as needed.

3 In a medium bowl, whisk together the flour, salt, baking soda, and cinnamon with a fork. Fold into the wet ingredients with a rubber spatula.

4 Add in the oats, cornflakes, and coconut, and stir to thoroughly combine so that all the mix-ins are suspended in the cookie dough.

5 Using a medium cookie scoop, about 1½ tablespoons of dough, scoop cookies onto a large plate.

6 Refrigerate the plate of scooped dough for 2 hours.

7 Preheat the oven to 350°F and line two baking sheets with parchment paper.

8 Transfer the cookie scoops onto the baking sheets, leaving a few inches between them.

9 Bake for 12 to 14 minutes, or until golden around the edges and soft in the center. Don't worry if they appear underbaked—they will firm up considerably as they cool.

10   Allow the cookies to rest on the baking sheets for 10 minutes before transferring to a wire rack to cool completely.

11   Serve or store at room temperature for up to 5 days.

LEMON CHEESECAKE TART WITH GINGERSNAP CRUST

MAKES ONE 9-INCH TART

CRUST

- 6 tablespoons unsalted butter
- 8 ounces gingersnap cookies (about 32 cookies)
- 1/8 teaspoon kosher salt
- 1 egg yolk

FILLING

- 8 ounces reduced-fat cream cheese, room temperature
- 2/3 cup 2% plain Greek yogurt
- 1/2 cup granulated sugar
- 3 large eggs
  Juice and zest of 1½ large lemons (¼ cup juice)
- 1/8 teaspoon kosher salt
- 2 cups prepared coconut whipped cream or fresh whipped cream for topping

Michael loves any lemon or lime dessert, and he likes a high lemon-to-sugar ratio for a flavor that is puckery and tart. This lemon cheesecake tart has become one of his favorites, reminiscent of both Key lime pie and cheesecake. The filling is made of cream cheese and Greek yogurt to achieve a base that is luscious and light without using the condensed milk that is usually called for in these types of desserts. The crust uses gingersnap cookies and marries beautifully with the bright, creamy filling. Because this tart must be made ahead, it's perfect for a dinner party and any hosting occasion.

1 **TO MAKE THE CRUST:** Melt the butter in a small skillet over medium heat. Continue to cook until it starts to turn brown and smells nutty. Turn off the heat.

2 Crush the cookies a bit in the palm of your hands and place in a food processor with the salt. Pulse until you have large crumbs.

3 Add the butter, then pulse a few more times until it resembles wet sand. Add the egg yolk and pulse again to combine.

4 Coat a 9-inch tart pan with a removable bottom with nonstick cooking spray.

5 Press the crust firmly into the pan using the bottom of a measuring cup, making sure it goes up the sides. Reserve whatever crumbs don't fit neatly into the pan for topping the finished tart.

6 Freeze the crust for about 10 minutes until solid. Meanwhile, preheat the oven to 325°F.

continues

7   Bake the crust for 20 minutes, then let it cool on a wire rack. Leave the oven on for the next step.

8   **WHILE THE CRUST COOLS, MAKE THE FILLING:** Combine the cream cheese, yogurt, and granulated sugar in the bowl of a food processor and process until the mixture is extremely smooth and well blended, a minute or two, scraping the sides as needed to fully incorporate. Add the eggs, lemon juice and zest, and salt and keep processing for about 10 seconds until very creamy.

9   Pour the filling into the cooled crust until it almost reaches the top, and bake until it is mostly set (a little jiggle is fine), 35 to 40 minutes.

10   Turn the oven off and open the door a crack. Let the tart sit in the oven this way for 15 minutes before transferring it to a wire rack on the counter to cool to room temperature. Refrigerate the tart for at least 1 hour to set completely. This slow cooling process prevents cracks on the surface, which can happen when there is a sudden temperature change.

11   After its time in the fridge, unmold the tart, spread whipped cream all over the top, sprinkle with the reserved gingersnap crumbs, and serve. Leftovers will keep for up to 5 days in the refrigerator.

EVEN FUDGIER AVOCADO BROWNIES

MAKES 9 LARGE OR 16 SMALL BROWNIES

½ cup unsweetened cocoa powder

1 teaspoon baking soda

½ teaspoon kosher salt

½ cup gluten-free all-purpose flour

1 large, ripe avocado, pitted and peeled

⅓ cup unsweetened creamy almond butter

¼ cup brewed coffee, cold

⅔ cup maple syrup

2 large eggs, room temperature

2 teaspoons vanilla extract

1 cup dark chocolate chips for mixing and topping

If you follow me on social media, you know my Fudgy Avocado Brownies. They became a bit legendary, and seemingly overnight people all over the world were making them. Since then, I've taken time to tweak them just a bit to improve on them: I wanted them higher in height, a little sweeter, and with a texture so fudgy that they would hold up in the fridge all week. Make sure to use ripe avocado—if it's too hard it won't blend easily into the batter, and we want the avocado to be invisible. This, my friends, is the new and final Fudgy Avocado Brownie.

1 Preheat the oven to 350°F.

2 Line an 8-inch square baking pan with parchment paper and spray with nonstick spray. In a large bowl, mix together the cocoa powder, baking soda, salt, and flour with a fork. Set aside.

3 To a high-speed blender, add the avocado, almond butter, coffee, maple syrup, eggs, and vanilla. Blend for about 30 seconds, scraping the sides as needed, until very smooth. You will taste any chunks of avocado, so blend well!

4 Add the avocado mixture to the dry ingredients and whisk until there are no more traces of flour. Mix ¾ cup of the chocolate chips into the batter, then transfer to the prepared pan.

5 Top the brownie batter with the remaining ¼ cup of chocolate chips.

6 Bake for 25 to 30 minutes until set. A tester should still come out a bit damp—you want them fudgy.

7 Cool in the pan for 15 minutes, then remove in one piece and place on a wire rack to finish cooling.

8 Cut into 9 or 12 pieces, depending on how large of a brownie you want. Dipping your knife into hot water between cuts helps ensure clean lines. Store the brownies in the refrigerator for up to a week or in the freezer for up to 3 months.

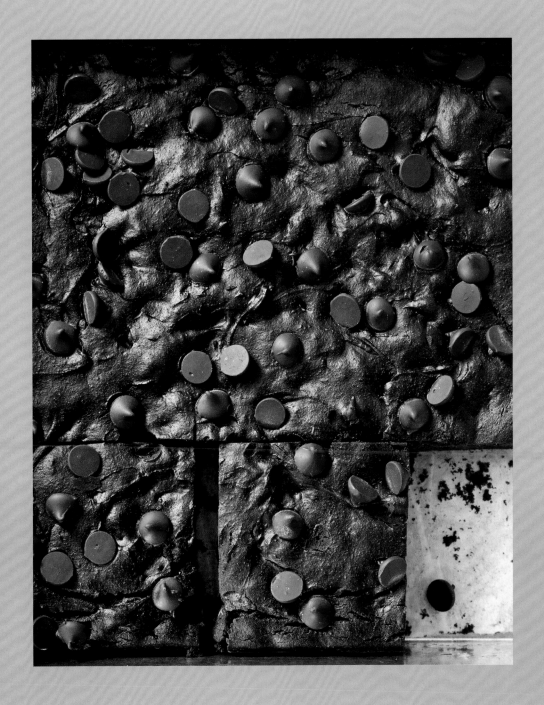

DARK CHOCOLATE EARL GREY MOUSSE

MAKES 6 SERVINGS

- 1 Earl Grey tea bag
- ¼ cup maple syrup
- 1 cup chopped dark chocolate
- ½ teaspoon vanilla extract
- ¼ teaspoon kosher salt
- 1 pound silken tofu

Coconut whipped cream for serving

Chocolate shavings for serving (optional)

Go figure that the one recipe I have in this book that involves tofu is a dessert.

I don't eat a lot of tofu, and when I do, it's usually in the form of a sweet and creamy mousse like this one. It's incredible how silken tofu will whip up in seconds and so closely mimic the cream and eggs used in a traditional mousse. The Earl Grey tea provides a subtle floral note that I love, and I always finish these with a bit of store-bought coconut whipped cream (which is also vegan). No one will ever believe there is tofu in their chocolate mousse.

1 In a small saucepan, bring ¾ cup of water to a boil.

2 Take the water off the heat and drop the tea bag in. Cover the saucepan with the lid and leave it to steep for 6 to 10 minutes. The longer the tea steeps, the more Earl Grey flavor you will have; 8 minutes will produce a subtle yet noticeable flavor. Remove the tea bag and bring the pot to a simmer again. Once again remove from the heat, add the maple syrup and chocolate, and stir to melt the chocolate.

3 Transfer the chocolate mixture to a high-speed blender and add the vanilla, salt, and tofu. Puree until completely smooth, stopping to scrape the sides of the blender with a rubber spatula as needed to fully incorporate.

4 Divide the mixture evenly among six ramekins and chill for at least 4 hours.

5 When serving, top the mousse with the whipped cream and chocolate shavings, if using.

CARROT SHEET CAKE WITH CINNAMON CREAM CHEESE FROSTING

MAKES ONE 9 BY 13-INCH SHEET CAKE

½ cup neutral oil

½ cup unsweetened applesauce

½ cup milk (any will work)

½ cup granulated sugar

½ cup packed light brown sugar

4 large eggs

1½ cups gluten-free all-purpose flour

1½ cups almond flour

1½ teaspoons ground cinnamon

¼ teaspoon ground cloves

½ teaspoon ground nutmeg

½ teaspoon ground ginger

2 teaspoons baking powder

1½ teaspoons baking soda

1 teaspoon kosher salt

3 cups grated carrots (4 to 6 carrots)

⅔ cup unsweetened shredded coconut

1 cup toasted walnuts, chopped

FROSTING

4 ounces ⅓-less-fat cream cheese

1 stick (½ cup) unsalted butter, room temperature

2 cups confectioners' sugar, sifted

½ teaspoon vanilla extract

¼ teaspoon ground cinnamon

¼ teaspoon kosher salt

½ cup toasted walnuts for topping

Please do not be put off by the number of ingredients in this cake—it couldn't be easier to make and after many trials I've deemed every last ingredient necessary. I mean . . . a super-moist carrot cake made in one bowl with no mixer required? Yes, please.

It also has half the sugar and fat of most other great carrot cake recipes, without any sacrifice in flavor or texture. I love using almond flour mixed with all-purpose flour to create a cake base that produces both a moist and fluffy crumb. Applesauce makes a lot of sense here as a substitute for some of the oil, marrying well with the carrot and warm spices. The frosting on this cake is halfway between a yogurt consistency and a buttercream due to the water content in reduced-fat cream cheese, and I love it this way. This recipe makes a larger cake perfect for serving a crowd or a small group and ensuring leftovers are waiting for you in the fridge. Be it Easter, Mother's Day, or a cozy fall Sunday afternoon, this carrot cake is always a crowd-pleaser.

1 Preheat the oven to 350°F. Spray a 9 by 13-inch baking dish with nonstick spray.

2 In a medium bowl, whisk together the oil, applesauce, milk, granulated sugar, brown sugar, and eggs.

3 To the wet ingredients, add the all-purpose flour, almond flour, cinnamon, cloves, nutmeg, ginger, baking powder, baking soda, and salt. Whisk until thoroughly combined and there are no traces of flour remaining.

4 Fold in the carrots, coconut, and walnuts.

5 Transfer the batter into the prepared pan and smooth the top.

6 Bake until the top is puffed, the cake is golden around the edges, and a toothpick comes out dry, 40 to 45 minutes.

continues

7 **TO PREPARE THE FROSTING:** While the cake is baking, remove the cream cheese from the refrigerator so it starts to soften. Set aside.

8 When the cake is done, transfer the pan to a wire rack and allow the cake to cool completely in the pan.

9 **TO MAKE THE FROSTING:** Put the cream cheese, which should be soft by now but not warm, in the bowl of a stand mixer fitted with the paddle attachment (or a mixing bowl, if using a hand mixer). If the cream cheese is too warm, it will result in a runny frosting because reduced-fat cream cheese has more liquid. Cream together the cream cheese and butter until just smooth, then add the confectioners' sugar, vanilla, cinnamon, and salt.

10 Beat the frosting until well mixed and fluffy.

11 Spread the frosting over the top of the cooled cake almost to the edges. Sprinkle walnuts along the border or in diagonal stripes, and refrigerate until ready to serve.

12 Serve, or store in the fridge for 3 to 4 days.

THE BEST VANILLA LAYER CAKE WITH STRAWBERRY JAM AND STRAWBERRY BUTTERCREAM

MAKES 10 TO 12 SERVINGS | ONE DOUBLE LAYER 8-INCH CAKE

2½ cups gluten-free all-purpose flour

¼ cup cornstarch

½ teaspoon baking soda

2 teaspoons baking powder

½ teaspoon kosher salt

1½ cups unsweetened almond milk (or cow's milk)

2 teaspoons apple cider vinegar

¾ cup coconut oil, room temperature

1 cup granulated sugar

1 tablespoon vanilla extract

4 large eggs, room temperature

STRAWBERRY BUTTERCREAM FROSTING

1½ cups freeze-dried strawberries

2 sticks (1 cup) vegan unsalted butter, room temperature (or regular butter if preferred)

3 cups confectioners' sugar

2 tablespoons unsweetened almond milk (or cow's milk)

1 teaspoon vanilla extract

¼ teaspoon kosher salt

½ cup reduced sugar strawberry preserves (I like Trader Joe's brand)

I bake my own cake on my birthday.

Why? Because I am particular about cake. Vanilla is my very favorite cake, and too many of the expensive ones you buy are very beautiful and very dry. I love frosting, but don't want too much frosting. I also like a touch of berry flavor, but not too much . . . I don't want a strawberry shortcake, where fruit is the star. I want cake to be the star. And I want a perfect cake at that. See why I make it myself?

This cake is a bit of a marvel. It's so tender and moist, with a deep vanilla flavor throughout and happens to be gluten and dairy free. The layer of jam inside is the perfect tart-sweet balance for the outer buttercream layer, which has a subtle strawberry flavor thanks to dried strawberries. Feel free to use regular butter in the frosting. You might soon find yourself making your own birthday cake from now on too . . . It's actually a lot more enjoyable than it sounds.

1 Preheat the oven to 350°F.

2 Line two 8-inch round cake pans with parchment paper and spray with nonstick cooking spray.

3 In a medium mixing bowl, combine the flour, cornstarch, baking soda, baking powder, and salt and sift to combine with a fork. To the measuring cup of milk, add the vinegar. Set both aside.

4 In the bowl of a stand mixer, or using a hand mixer, beat together the coconut oil and granulated sugar on medium-high until light and fluffy, about 3 minutes. Add the vanilla and eggs and beat for 30 seconds more. Add half of the flour mixture and mix on low speed until incorporated, then add half of the milk mixture and mix until just incorporated. Add the remaining half of the flour mixture, then the milk mixture as before and beat to combine again.

continues

The Best Vanilla Layer Cake with Strawberry Jam
and Strawberry Buttercream
CONTINUED

5   Split the batter evenly into the prepared pans (using a scale makes this easy) and bake for 28 to 34 minutes, or until the cake is lightly golden brown and springs back when pressed. Take the cakes out of the oven and transfer them in their pans to a wire rack for 15 to 20 minutes. Turn the cakes out of their pans, peel off the parchment, and allow to cool completely before frosting.

6   **TO MAKE THE STRAWBERRY BUTTERCREAM FROSTING:** Add the freeze-dried strawberries to a small blender or food processor and pulse until they form a very fine powder, giving you about ¾ cup of crumbs. You can also do this with a plastic bag and rolling pin. Set aside.

7   In a stand mixer fitted with the whisk attachment, beat the softened butter until creamy, about 1 minute. Add ½ cup of the powdered strawberries and beat on low for a few seconds to combine.

8   Scrape down the bowl and add the confectioners' sugar, milk, vanilla, and salt. Beat for 1 minute to combine, scraping down the sides as needed. The frosting will be a pastel pink color.

9   Trim off the very tops of your cakes with a serrated knife to allow them to lay flat.

10   Place your first cake layer on your cake stand or serving dish. Pipe a circle of frosting around the outer edge of the top of the cake. In a random pattern, pipe frosting into the middle of the cake, then smooth out the middle of the frosting with a spatula, keeping the edge of the frosting intact and taller than the middle. (Basically you're making a bed to keep the jam inside the cake.) Fill with the strawberry preserves, spreading it evenly onto the cake.

11   Place the second layer of cake on top of the preserves. Frost the top and outside, smoothing as you go. Top the cake with the remaining ¼ cup of strawberry powder and serve. Leftovers will stay moist, cut sides wrapped in plastic wrap and covered, for 3 to 4 days, getting a bit drier each day from baking.

ORANGE RICOTTA COMPANY CAKE

MAKES ONE LOAF

3 large eggs, room temperature

¾ cup whole-milk ricotta cheese

¼ cup neutral oil

1 teaspoon vanilla extract

¾ cup granulated sugar

2 tablespoons orange zest (from about 3 oranges)

½ cup fresh orange juice (from about 2 oranges)

1¾ cups gluten-free all-purpose flour

½ teaspoon kosher salt

2 teaspoons baking powder

½ teaspoon baking soda

GLAZE

1 tablespoon fresh orange juice

½ cup confectioners' sugar

Pinch of salt

Everyone needs a company cake recipe: the sort of cake you make in one bowl, that freezes well, and that you can whip up at a moment's notice. This is my company cake, though it's so delicious and simple to make that I make it whether visitors are over or not. I keep the sugar in check with a cake that isn't too sweet, but if you like a very sweet cake, increase it to 1 cup . . . and there is just enough sugar in the glaze to do its job. With a fraction of the oil of most loaf cakes, it's not very heavy—meaning that a slice with afternoon tea won't have you struggling to get off the couch later. I can also attest that this cake is beautiful with any citrus: Lemon and grapefruit are favorites at my house as well.

1 Preheat the oven to 350°F.

2 Grease one standard loaf pan with nonstick spray and line it with a parchment paper sling for easy removal.

3 In a large bowl, whisk together the eggs and ricotta until blended. Add the oil, vanilla, granulated sugar, orange zest and juice, and whisk again to combine.

4 Add the flour, salt, baking powder, and baking soda and whisk until there are no traces of flour visible. The batter will be lumpy even now, but it'll just be the curds of ricotta.

5 Pour the batter into the prepared pan and bake until puffed, and golden, 50 to 60 minutes. Let the loaf cool for 15 minutes in the pan before turning out onto a wire rack to cool completely.

6 **WHILE THE CAKE COOLS, MAKE THE GLAZE:** In a small bowl, whisk together the orange juice, confectioners' sugar, and salt. Cover and set aside until you are ready to glaze.

7 Using a pastry brush or spoon, cover the cake with the glaze, going over and over the cake until it is used up. Let the glaze harden for at least 5 minutes, then serve.

SWEET POTATO CUPCAKES WITH SALTED MAPLE FROSTING

MAKES 12 CUPCAKES

1¼ cups gluten-free all-purpose flour

½ cup almond flour

½ teaspoon ground ginger

1 teaspoon ground cinnamon

¼ teaspoon ground nutmeg

1 teaspoon kosher salt

2 teaspoons baking powder

1 teaspoon baking soda

1½ cups cooked sweet potato (2 to 3 sweet potatoes)

3 large eggs, room temperature

½ cup granulated sugar

¼ cup maple syrup

¼ cup neutral oil (light olive oil, sunflower oil, vegetable oil)

SALTED MAPLE FROSTING

½ cup unsalted butter, softened

1¼ cups confectioners' sugar, sifted

2 tablespoons maple syrup

½ teaspoon salt

When I roast sweet potatoes for dinner or a salad, I always make a double batch. I love using sweet potato the next night in soups and tacos, or even, if they are large enough, cut open and filled with spicy chickpeas and tahini. One day, I decided to use them in place of pumpkin in some muffins. Then I thought, "Maybe I'll make cupcakes with a salted maple buttercream frosting as an after-school treat for the kids . . ." and thus these cupcakes were born. They are quick to throw together with leftover sweet potato, but you can also substitute canned pumpkin if that's what you have. They're fluffy, filled with warm spices, and topped with a luscious maple frosting, making them the perfect sweet treat on any blustery fall day.

1 Preheat the oven to 350°F.

2 Spray the cups of a standard 12-cup muffin tin with nonstick spray, or use muffin liners and spray the insides of those.

3 In a large bowl, whisk together the all-purpose flour, almond flour, ginger, cinnamon, nutmeg, salt, baking powder, and baking soda.

4 Remove the sweet potato flesh from the skins and add the flesh to a high-speed blender. Add in the eggs, granulated sugar, maple syrup, and oil and blend for 10 seconds until very smooth.

5 Add the wet ingredients to the bowl of dry ingredients and mix until there are no streaks of flour visible.

6 Transfer the batter evenly into the muffin cups. An ice cream scoop is the right size.

7 Bake for 20 to 25 minutes until a tester comes out just clean.

8 Cool the cupcakes for 10 minutes in the pan before transferring to a rack to cool completely.

9   **WHILE THE CUPCAKES COOL, MAKE THE SALTED MAPLE FROSTING:** Add the butter to the bowl of a standing mixer and beat for 1 to 2 minutes to aerate. Add half of the confectioners' sugar along with the maple syrup and salt. Continue to mix to incorporate. Add the rest of the confectioners' sugar to the bowl and beat until light and fluffy.

10   Spread or pipe the frosting onto the cooled cupcakes and serve. Serve or refrigerate for up to 5 days.

SALTED PALEO BLONDIES

MAKES 9 LARGE OR 16 SMALL BLONDIES

2   large eggs

½   cup unsweetened creamy cashew
    or almond butter

¼   cup coconut oil, melted and cooled

¾   cup coconut sugar

½   teaspoon vanilla extract

⅓   cup coconut flour

1½ cups almond flour

½   teaspoon baking soda

½   teaspoon kosher salt

1   cup dark chocolate chips
    (dairy-free for strict paleo diets)

    Flaky sea salt for topping

These blondies are one of the first successful sweet recipes I created after having kids. I was learning to incorporate more naturally gluten- and dairy-free ingredients and working more with unrefined sugar. I have loosened up my view since then on refined sugar and dairy, but these are still the blondies I make again and again, because they are just so rich, chewy, and delicious. No one would ever guess they were paleo unless you told them.

1   Preheat the oven to 325°F.

2   Line an 8-inch square pan with parchment paper so you have an overhang on two sides and spray with nonstick cooking spray.

3   In a medium bowl, whisk together the eggs, nut butter, coconut oil, coconut sugar, and vanilla to combine.

4   Using a rubber spatula, fold in the coconut flour, almond flour, baking soda, and salt. Stir to combine. Fold in the chocolate chips.

5   Spread the mixture into the prepared pan, smooth the top, and sprinkle with a pinch of flaky salt. Bake the blondies for 18 to 22 minutes, or until the center is just slightly soft and the edges have started to brown. Don't overbake—the blondies will firm up as they cool.

6   Let the blondies cool in the pan on a wire rack for 30 minutes, then lift them out of the pan using the paper. Allow them to cool completely on the rack before cutting into squares.

7   Serve, and store leftovers at room temperature for up to 5 days.

SECRET
WEAPONS

BASIL WALNUT PESTO

MAKES 1½ CUPS

3   tablespoons walnuts

2   large garlic cloves, smashed

2   cups fresh basil leaves

¼   teaspoon kosher salt

½   cup extra-virgin olive oil

½   cup freshly grated Parmesan
     cheese

You may not need a recipe for pesto if you have a culinarily gifted Nonna, but for the rest of us it helps to have some guardrails. Pine nuts are traditional in pesto, but walnuts are cheaper, more easily accessible, and a perfectly worthy substitute here. When summer basil is abundant, I make big batches of this pesto and freeze them in ice cube trays to be transferred to freezer bags. This means that in the dead of winter I am never far from this sharp, buttery, herbaceous sauce that brings me right back to summer.

In a small sauté pan set over medium-low heat, toast the walnuts for 3 to 5 minutes until golden brown and fragrant. Coarsely chop the walnuts and transfer to a plate to come to room temperature. In the bowl of a food processor, process the garlic until coarsely chopped, about 10 seconds. Add the basil leaves and salt and blend for about 30 seconds until homogenous. With the motor running, pour the olive oil through the feed tube and process until the pesto is thoroughly blended. Open the bowl to add the Parmesan, then process for a minute more. The pesto will keep for up to 1 week in the fridge.

THREE WAYS TO USE BASIL WALNUT PESTO

✳ *Add to a sauté pan and toss with warm pasta and more Parmesan cheese*

✳ *As the base of a salad dressing, shaken in a jar with equal parts olive oil and vinegar*

✳ *To top spaghetti squash, grilled chicken, or shrimp*

FRESH
BREAD CRUMBS

MAKES 1½ CUPS

2 cups stale bread (from Three-Year Gluten-Free Bread [page 192], or any hearty country bread you have)

This is a basic recipe for quick, fresh bread crumbs to use in place of store-bought. I always have bread crumbs on hand, and now you can too. Anytime I have a bit of bread left over, and not enough for a meal, into the food processor it goes. The fresh bread crumbs will last, refrigerated, for about 3 days or frozen for up to 3 months. You can also give them a sauté in a pan with olive oil or bake them in the oven until golden brown for dried bread crumbs that are better for you and cheaper than anything you'll find in the store.

1 Cut the bread into 1- to 2-inch cubes. Place in a food processor or high-powered blender and process until you have crumbs. Stop the processor and scrape the sides when needed to ensure the bread processes evenly.

2 Store in the refrigerator for up to 1 week.

THREE WAYS TO USE FRESH BREAD CRUMBS

* *As part of a filling for meatloaf and meatballs of all kinds*

* *Sauté in olive oil and use as a crunchy salad topper*

* *To cover baked pastas, vegetables, and gratins*

ONE-INGREDIENT BALSAMIC GLAZE

MAKES ½ CUP

1   cup balsamic vinegar

If you look at the ingredients on a bottle of balsamic glaze, it's almost always a lot more than balsamic vinegar, but that is all you need to make it yourself. This version has no added sugar, no ingredients you can't pronounce—just syrupy, tart deliciousness whose sweetness comes from the balsamic itself. Note that when the vinegar is boiling, the fumes will float into the air (that means it's working!), so you might need have a pair of glasses handy in case the fumes irritate your eyes.

1   Pour the balsamic into a small saucepan set over medium-low heat.

2   Bring it to a low boil, then turn the heat to low to keep it at a simmer for 12 to 15 minutes, depending on the size of your pan. Stir occasionally until the balsamic is reduced by half and lightly coats the back of a spoon. It will thicken more as it cools. Transfer to a mason jar or other airtight container, let cool to room temperature, then cover and refrigerate for 3 to 4 weeks.

THREE WAYS TO USE BALSAMIC GLAZE

*   *Drizzle on a salad. Anything with tomato or cheese is a foolproof pairing.*

*   *Serve in a little dish with fresh berries. Strawberries in particular are wonderful—it's like a highbrow version of chocolate-covered strawberries.*

*   *Spoon over grilled chicken or steak*

QUICK PICKLED RED ONIONS

MAKES 6 SERVINGS ✳ 1 (16-OUNCE) JAR

1 cup apple cider vinegar

1 tablespoon cane sugar

1 tablespoon sea salt

2 medium red onions

1 garlic clove, halved and smashed (optional)

½ teaspoon mixed peppercorns (pink or black; optional)

I love having a jar of these in the refrigerator to wake up a variety of dishes. They are tart and slightly sweet, and they turn a stunning magenta color that makes every dish look just a bit prettier. I love using peppercorns in here too, particularly pink ones, which add a subtle floral note, but don't go to the store for them. These onions are delightful even without pink peppercorns.

1 Bring 1 cup of water to a boil in a tea kettle or on the stovetop. Add the apple cider vinegar, cane sugar, and sea salt to a 16-ounce glass jar.

2 Add the hot water to the jar and stir quickly to dissolve the sugar. Let cool to room temperature.

3 Thinly slice the onions (with a knife or using a mandoline) and add to the jar. Place the garlic and peppercorns, if using, in the jar, nestling them in among the onions. Store the onions in the fridge.

4 Your pickled onions will be ready to eat once they're bright pink and tender—about 2 hours depending on the thickness of the onions.

5 They will keep in the fridge for up to 2 weeks.

THREE WAYS TO USE PICKLED ONIONS

✳ *As a fish, chicken, or beef taco topping*

✳ *Tossed into a grain bowl or grain salad*

✳ *As a topping for avocado toast and fried eggs*

SHALLOT-HERB COMPOUND BUTTER

MAKES 8 SERVINGS

1   medium shallot, peeled

½   cup (1 stick) unsalted butter, room temperature

1   tablespoon chopped fresh thyme

2   tablespoons finely minced fresh parsley

¼   teaspoon freshly cracked black pepper

½   teaspoon fine sea salt

Just a few additions to a stick of butter make it instantly feel special. The possibilities are greater than I could possibly list here, so take this classic shallot-and-herb combination and get the feel of it before playing around with other additions such as citrus peel, peppercorns, roasted garlic, and more.

1   Grate the shallot using a microplane. In a small bowl and using a fork, mash the butter with the grated shallot, thyme, parsley, pepper, and salt.

2   Spoon the butter mixture onto a piece of parchment paper or plastic wrap, form into a log, and roll it up tightly. Chill for at least 3 hours before using, and store in the refrigerator for up to 5 days or freeze for up to 6 months.

THREE WAYS TO USE SHALLOT-HERB COMPOUND BUTTER

✳ *Top a warm steak with a slice and allow it to melt (my go-to)*

✳ *Serve with good bread for dinner*

✳ *Toss with cooked broccoli, green beans, or carrots*

SLOW-ROASTED TOMATOES

MAKES 6 SERVINGS

1½ pounds (a little more than 3 cups) cherry tomatoes, halved

¼ cup extra-virgin olive oil

1 teaspoon kosher salt

5 garlic cloves, unpeeled

Even out of season, grocery store tomatoes transform into ruby-red gems of deep sweetness when cooked very low, and very slow, in the oven. Three hours of roasting time sounds like a lot, and it is, but you can go about your business, as they need no hands-on time while they roast. These are so very satisfying to make—a great plan for a lazy Sunday afternoon.

1 Preheat the oven to 225°F.

2 On a large sheet pan, toss the tomatoes with the olive oil, salt, and garlic.

3 Roast for 3 hours, untouched. When finished, the tomatoes should be shriveled, intensely flavored, and sweet. Once out of the oven, peel and discard the garlic skins and smash the garlic a bit.

4 Use straight away, refrigerate for up to 1 week, or freeze for up to 6 months.

THREE WAYS TO USE SLOW-ROASTED TOMATOES

* *Toss into pasta with a generous drizzle of olive oil, basil, and Parmesan for an instant, rustic sauce*

* *Top my white bean hummus (page 73) or another legume dip for a beautiful presentation*

* *Spoon onto toast smeared with good ricotta or goat cheese*

GREEN FRIDGE SAUCE

MAKES 1 CUP

1 cup mixed fresh herbs (such as parsley, cilantro, dill, basil, tarragon, and chives)

3 green onions, white and green parts

2 garlic cloves, minced

Juice of ½ lemon

1 tablespoon apple cider vinegar

½ teaspoon kosher salt

¼ teaspoon freshly cracked black pepper

⅓ to ½ cup extra-virgin olive oil

At least one if not two "fridge sauces" sit in lidded jars in my refrigerator door at all times. When dinner comes around and I don't have the energy to think of a "recipe," I pick a main course ingredient and grab a sauce, comforted that the work is done for me. Use parsley, cilantro, dill, basil, tarragon, or chives. Parsley in particular is a nice base herb as it goes so well with others. The other ingredients are usually those I have in my pantry.

1 Finely chop the herbs and green onions and add them to a bowl. Stir in the garlic, lemon juice, apple cider vinegar, salt, and pepper. Slowly whisk in the oil.

2 **FOOD PROCESSOR METHOD:** Give the mixed herbs, green onions, and garlic, a rough chop and put these along with the rest of the ingredients in a food processor and pulse to blend well. Or use an immersion blender. Taste, and adjust seasonings to your liking. Serve at room temperature or store in the fridge for up to 1 week.

THREE WAYS TO USE GREEN FRIDGE SAUCE

✶ *Toss with a can of drained chickpeas and add it to a green salad*

✶ *Spoon it over grilled, pan-seared, or roasted fish*

✶ *Drizzle on warm roasted or boiled potatoes*

ACKNOWLEDGMENTS

/
THIS BOOK
WOULD
STILL BE A
DREAM
IF IT WASN'T
FOR ALL OF
YOU.
/

This book would still be a dream if it wasn't for all of you.

My readers and social media family: Thank you for trusting me into your homes, hearts, and bellies and being so very open to what I have to offer you. Thank you for being willing to eat a salad with a spoon.

Dervla Kelly, my incredible editor, whose patience, professionalism, and wisdom steered my writing. I immediately knew I was in the best of hands.

Thank you to the whole Penguin Random House team that quite literally brought *Big Bites* to life: Stephanie Huntwork, Mia Johnson, Laura Palese, Ashley Pierce, Katherine Leak, Heather Williamson, and Jonathan Sung. From art direction and design to copyediting to marketing and publicity, your efforts and investments in this book are so very appreciated.

To my literary agents at Fletcher & Co., Christy Fletcher and Lisa Grubka, for seeing this book before I saw it myself and making me feel supported from start to finish.

My beloved photographer, Christine Han: I knew you were something special when you played Brittany Spears in the kitchen years ago to get me comfortable dancing on camera. You really get me, and are insanely talented to boot. You, along with photo assistant Alex Medina and prop stylists Maeve Sheridan and Ashleigh Sarbone, brought such vibrance and vitality to every subject photographed. I sometimes look at these photos and think . . . This is *my* food?

Well, it sort of is.

To Barrett Washburne, along with Lauren Radel, thank you for your gorgeous food styling, warmth, and friendship. I am convinced that no other duo could make these recipes look better. All you had to hear was "I want it to feel impossible not to eat this food" and you got to work. The professional way you run a kitchen almost fooled me into believing you never break from your all-business approach. Fortunately for me, you are as skilled in humor as you are in cooking. What fun we had.

Laura Arnold, my priceless recipe tester, you plowed through 120 recipes with generous positivity and wisdom. Opening up one's recipes to critique can feel intimidating, and your can-do attitude brought a feeling of warmth and friendship to the process. You are an absolute gem.

Thank you to my chef instructors at Ice Culinary in NYC for showing me that I wasn't actually a great cook . . . yet. You knocked out the bad habits and built me back up as a student and cook at the ripe age of 28.

Thank you to Martha Stewart and the whole Martha Show team for taking a chance on me fresh out of culinary school, and undoubtedly setting the tone for what would become this lifelong career of mine.

To Heather Reisman, who showed me what it looked like to take risks in business and a risk on myself. Your curiosity and ability to envision what could be is contagious.

Thank you to my manager, Denise, who is the closest I've come to having a true partner in my business. Entrepreneurship can feel lonely, and you stepping in with your practical wisdom and graceful hustle has elevated the whole thing. I appreciate you.

Thank you to my dear friend Claire, aka my culinary soul sister. From making arancini together in culinary school to modern day phone calls ranting about the pitfalls of cast-iron pans and "is truffle oil even good?"—I appreciate your friendship and support beyond measure.

To my mom, you made space for my eager exploration in the kitchen as a child and continue to keep me wondering, questioning, and pushing myself to view my food from another point of view. I love talking about food with you and most anything else. My favorite memories are around a kitchen table, or picnic table, or beach blanket eating and laughing and enjoying the precious everyday moments of family. When I was a child, you supported me finding my way through food creation, one mess at a time. When you let me help in the kitchen you'd say, "why thank you, Kathleen, I could have done it in half the time without you!" Thanks for not being in a rush.

To my mini muffins, William and Caroline: your powdered sugar hands and sauce-stained shirts are my favorite part of our kitchen (even when I don't act like it). You motivate me every day to be the kind of cook that makes it fun and the kind of mom that makes you proud.

To my darling Michael, I love you for many reasons, your steadfast belief in me is just one of them. Thank you for eating my food, day in and day out, and still thinking it's good.

INDEX